MW00721026

HTML 4.0

Addison-Wesley
Nitty Gritty

PROGRAMMING SERIES

HTML 4.0

Ingo Dellwig

ADDISON-WESLEY

An imprint of Pearson Education

Boston • San Francisco • New York • Toronto • Montreal • London • Munich
Paris • Madrid • Cape Town • Sydney • Tokyo • Singapore • Mexico City

PEARSON EDUCATION LIMITED

Head Office
Edinburgh Gate, Harlow, Essex CM20 2JE
Tel: +44 (0)1279 623623 Fax: +44 (0)1279 431059

London Office
128 Long Acre, London WC2E 9AN
Tel: +44 (0)20 7447 2000 Fax: +44 (0)20 7240 5771
Websites:
www.it-minds.com   www.aw.com/cseng

First published in Great Britain 2002
© Pearson Education Limited 2002

First published in 2000 as *HTML 4 Nitty Gritty* by Addison Wesley
Verlag, Germany.

The rights of Ingo Dellwig to be identified as Author of this Work have been
asserted by him in accordance with the Copyright, Designs and Patents Act 1988.

Library of Congress Cataloguing Publication Data
Applied for.

British Library Cataloguing in Publication Data
A CIP catalogue record for this book can be obtained from the British Library.

ISBN 0-201-75877-6

All rights reserved. No part of this publication may be reproduced, stored in a
retrieval system, or transmitted, in any form, or by any means, electronic, mechan-
ical, photocopying, recording or otherwise, without prior permission, in writing,
from the publisher.

The programs in this book have been included for their instructional value. The
publisher does not offer any warranties or representations in respect of their fit-
ness for a particular purpose, nor does the publisher accept any liability for any
loss or damage arising from their use.

10 9 8 7 6 5 4 3 2 1

Translated and typeset by Berlitz GlobalNET (UK) Ltd. of Luton, Bedfordshire.
Printed and bound in Great Britain by Biddles Ltd. of Guildford and King's Lynn.

The publishers' policy is to use paper manufactured from sustainable forests.

Contents

Part II – Take that!　　　　75

Preface

Dear Reader,

The development of the Internet and consequently the further development of Internet languages and technologies continues at a breakneck pace. The Hypertext Markup Language (HTML) version 4.0 has of course been on the market for some time. Only now does this language seem to have reached its point of maturity and lies at the cutting edge of technology.

Only the varied assortment of browsers, each supporting different standards, make it difficult for HTML programmers to create compatible HTML sites. For this reason you will find a comprehensive quick reference section in this book which documents the compatibility of each tag and its attributes with diverse browsers.

If you have no experience with HTML the introduction will help get you started. Here you will learn how to program in easy-to-understand steps. In the introduction you will get to know the basic HTML technologies. With the help of the quick reference section you will be able to build your knowledge up to a professional level.

Finally I would like to draw your attention to a couple of interesting technologies (style sheets, Dynamic HTML etc.) detailed in the "Tips and tricks" section that are not directly connected with HTML 4.0 but make the life of an HTML programmer that much easier.

At this point I would like to thank all those who contributed (in whatever way) to the creation of this book:

Firstly I must mention Christina Gibbs, the editor at Addison-Wesley, who pulled out all the stops to allow me more time to write this book.

Further thanks goes to my brother Elmar Dellwig who took on a greater share of the production work on "JavaScript 1.3", the tandem title in the Addison-Wesley Nitty Gritty series, than was originally planned.

I mustn't forget my parents and friends who hardly saw me during the "white-hot" creative phase. Sorry, things will calm down again now - promise!

Last but not least, I would like to thank the members of the Dortmund University Orchestra for being so thoughtful when I was immersed in my writing during our concert tour of Tuscany. Once again it was great fun touring with the orchestra.

Well, I hope you enjoy reading the book and that you find in it all the information you need about HTML 4.

Ingo Dellwig

Ingo Dellwig

... is an enthusiastic and dedicated Internet user who has had his own homepage for several years. He has been working with computers since 1986. His part-time work on the hotline of a major online service provider enabled him to gather experience with the Internet, while at the same time completing his Computer Studies course at the University of Dortmund. During this time, he was frequently confronted with the problems encountered by users in creating their own homepages. He became self-employed in 1997 and founded SPECTROsoftware, a software house that creates homepages for companies in a variety of industries, as well as working on projects in the entertainment sector and providing training courses.

"In my books I want to help the reader overcome their fear of theory by leading them step by step towards their goal using practical examples."

Ingo Dellwig seems to have been pretty successful with this approach. He has already written numerous books covering various aspects of the Internet, hardware and programming which have all been well received.

Part I

Start up!

Introduction

This book is divided into three sections. In the introduction you will learn about the basics of HTML programming and make yourself familiar with the most important tags. The quick reference section is designed to give you an overview of HTML 4 tags and serves as a quick look up. The tips and tricks section rounds off the book teaching you some of the tricks that you might perhaps not be aware of. There you will also find pointers to advanced languages and methods including, for example, a short introduction to Dynamic HTML and style sheets.

1.1 What is HTML?

Since you are holding a book with the title "HTML 4" in your hands I assume you already know what HTML is. Therefore I will not dwell too long on this point. The acronym HTML stands for "Hypertext Markup Language". This language enables the transmission and representation of Internet pages in the World Wide Web (WWW). Individual pages are navigated by means of links. Thus a click on a keyword or a graphic brings you to the next page. The whole www can be searched in this way.

Another important aspect of HTML is that it's universal. As HTML pages are saved in ASCII or text format they can be processed on almost any computer. A PC is therefore just as good in this respect as a Macintosh, a Unix system or even a handheld PC.

1.2 Requirements

If we want to program in HTML we'll need some tools all of which we can get for nothing. Firstly we have to generate the source code. To do this we need a text editor. Secondly it's important to check the results and to correct any mistakes. This will require a browser (or even better several browsers).

1.2.1 Text editor

In every operating system you'll find a text editor. In Windows for example you can use Notepad. Under Unix and Linux you have joe and the Macintosh also comes with its own text editor called SimpleText. The important thing is that your editor can save standard texts. You don't have to save any additional control commands such as bold, tables or justify. If your editor can do this then it is well suited for HTML programming.

1.2.2 Browser

A browser converts HTML code into a formatted Internet page, which it displays on the screen. There are many different browsers which interpret certain commands differently. However only two programs have really held their own against the competition. One is Internet Explorer from Microsoft and the other is Netscape Communicator from Netscape.

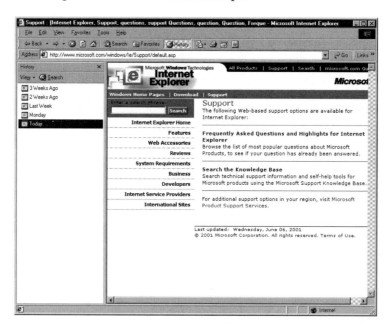

Figure 1.1 *Microsoft Internet Explorer 5.01*

This browser is preinstalled in the current Microsoft operating systems. If you are using another system you can download the latest version from the Internet. The address is:

www.microsoft.com/windows/ie/

Figure 1.2 *Netscape 6.0*

You can download this browser from the Internet at the following address:

www.netscape.com

In this book I will concentrate on these two browsers and list the differences between them as we deal with each topic. I'd like to use the following graphic to demonstrate that it's really sufficient to restrict ourselves to these two programs:

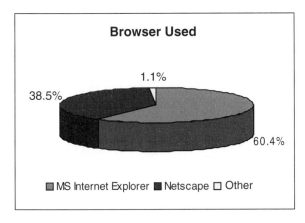

Figure 1.3 *Browser usage at WebHits.de (status 29.05.2000)*

START UP!

1.3 The basics of HTML

In this chapter I want to introduce you to working with HTML. You'll create your first HTML file, save and then view it. In addition you'll learn about the most important tags needed to create Internet pages using HTML.

1.3.1   Hello World!

From time immemorial it has been customary to greet the world when programming for the first time in a new programming language. So we'll output the text Hello World! to the screen. If this text appears on the screen then you have successfully generated and executed your first program. Right let's get to work ...

Start your favorite text editor and enter the following lines:

```
<html>
Hello World!
</html>
```

The tag <html> marks the HTML part of the document. For us to be able to look at the result we must save the source text to the hard disk. To do this I am now going to ask you to create a directory called HTML4 on your hard disk. Then save our first document in the file HelloWorld.html.

Tip Note that the source text must be saved in text format. If you save a HTML document in Word format, for example, additional control characters will be saved which make a HTML file unusable.

Figure 1.4 *HTML files are always saved in text format*

Our masterpiece is now on your hard disk. But how do we look at the result? If you have got an Internet browser installed such as Microsoft Internet Explorer or Netscape Communicator, you can open your file via the file manager (i.e. Windows Explorer) by means of a simple double click.

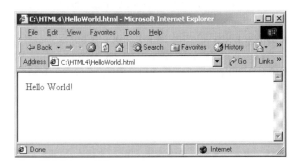

Figure 1.5 *This is how HelloWorld.html looks in Internet Explorer*

You've now written your first HTML file and displayed it in the browser. And you've met the two identifiers that distinguish an HTML file from other text files. One is the file extension `.htm` or `.html` and the other is the enclosing of the HTML code using the tags `<html>` and `</html>`. What exactly are these tags?

1.3.2 Tags

If, for instance, you want to display a section of text in bold the browser needs to know where the bold text begins and where it ends. To do this you must mark a start and an end point in the text. Bold text is indicated in HTML by the tag `<b>`.

By now you will certainly have noticed that tags are distinguished from normal text by pointed brackets (< and >). When you want to turn off the bold again use a closing tag. To distinguish this from the opening tag <b> a slash (/) is used. The end of a passage in boldface is therefore identified by </b>. Here is a specially adapted example:

```
<html>
This text is still formatted normally whereas the next three
words <b>appear in bold</b> on the screen.
</html>
```

Let's take a look at the result in the browser:

Figure 1.6 *As expected the selected words actually appear in bold*

1.3.3   Head and body

HTML pages can be split into two parts. The first is called the head and is identified by <head>. Since the head encloses an area this too will have a closing tag </head>. Everything you put in the head of an HTML page will not appear directly on the page but is noticeable in other ways. For instance you ought to select a title for your homepage. This will be displayed in most browsers in the title bar next to the browser name. The title is enclosed by <title> and </title>.

For every head there is a body. The HTML body contains all the information you want displayed directly on the page. The body is enclosed by <body> and </body>. If we give the HelloWorld code a head and body the source text will look like this:

```
<html>
  <head>
    <title>HelloWorld-Title</title>
  </head>
  <body>
    Hello World!
  </body>
</html>
```

Now the words "HelloWorld-Title" appear in the title bar.

Figure 1.7 *The title bar now contains the text enclosed by <title> and </title>*

1.3.4   Attributes

In many cases tags alone are insufficient. Let's assume we want to insert a horizontal rule into a document. We do that by using the tag `<hr>`. By default browsers provide horizontal rules in 3D effect with a shadow though sometimes we don't want this effect. So instead of inserting an additional tag to prevent the shadow we give the tag the suffix `noshade`. The way to write such a tag with an attribute is then `<hr  noshade>`. This will then produce a horizontal rule without a shadow.

In addition in the case of many attributes there is the option of assigning values. If we want to reduce the width of our rule by half then the attribute `width` is appropriate. Using `<hr width>` makes no sense though since the browser cannot tell we want a rule exactly half the default length. Therefore we assign `width` the value `50%` as follows: `<hr width= 50% >`. The rule will then be displayed at half the width.

You can also combine attributes. The tag `<hr noshade width=50%>` creates a rule with no shadow across half the width of the screen. The following screenshot provides an example of the four horizontal rule formats described above:

START UP!

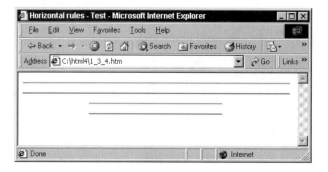

Figure 1.8 *The four horizontal rule formats*

There is not much more you need to know about HTML syntax. You now know about tags and their attributes. Now it's time to apply this knowledge and to learn about the various HTML tags.

1.4 Text formatting

For the most part an HTML page consists of normal text. So it doesn't look too dull and to highlight particular areas of text HTML gives you the facility to format the text in a creative way.

1.4.1 Line breaks and paragraphs

When you're copying simple continuous text into HTML code you will soon realize that there are no blank spaces at the beginning of a line nor line breaks or paragraphs. The browser always assumes that it has to insert new text after the previous word. It doesn't matter whether this word was several lines back. The advantage of this is that you can fit a text into different browsers whose display areas may differ. However when you need to insert line breaks you must create these with the tag `<br/>` (break). To avoid having to use blank lines with just the `<br/>` tag, another tag `<p>` (paragraph) was adopted to produce a paragraph. Since a line break doesn't mark an area but just a point, this is what is known as an 'empty' tag. You can also use `<p>` as a stand-alone tag although enclosing a paragraph by `<p>` and `</p>` is possible and indeed commonplace.

1.4.2 Umlauts and special characters

There are still unfortunately some old browsers around that will not accept umlauts in the source text. Later browsers though will recognize these special characters. If you want to make your page easily readable for all Internet users you should note that you can also produce umlauts using character references. In

HTML for example the letter ö is defined by the character reference `&ouml;`. The `&` tells you to expect a following character reference which always ends with a semicolon. The `o` says which vowel is involved and `uml` is an abbreviation for umlaut. The `&` and ß are represented by a character reference as the ß is another typical German letter and the `&` is reserved for identifying character references themselves. The symbols `<` and `>` are also reserved special characters. They are used to identify tags. We therefore have the following table:

Umlaut	Character reference
ä	ä
ö	ö
ü	ü
Ä	Ä
Ö	Ö
Ü	Ü
ß	ß
&	&
<	<
>	>

Table 1.1 *The most important character references for special characters*

You will find further character references for special characters in Appendix A. Here's a small sample text using character references for special characters:

```
<html>
  <head>
    <title>Special characters</title>
  </head>
  <body>
    This sample text is intended to show how special charac-
ters
    can be represented.<p>For instance note here how
    to insert the greater-than sign (&gt;)
    in HTML text.
  </body>
</html>
```

If we now take a look at this page we see the following output:

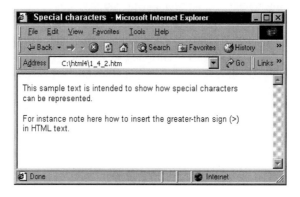

Figure 1.9 *Now the text reads as normal again*

Tip Since we'll not be working with such old browsers, which certainly wouldn't support HTML 4, I'll not use character references to represent umlauts in the examples that follow.

Nevertheless it's important for you to know what is going on when you read the source text of others. If you do want to use special characters that are reserved for HTML itself the only option is to force this by using character references.

1.4.3 Headings

For an HTML page to be clear it's necessary to type in headings and to make these stand out. There are a number of easy-to-handle tags which will do this. For the main heading you should use `<h1>` (heading). For the subheadings you've got the tags `<h2>` to `<h6>`. A heading is obviously a text area. Therefore closing tags will again be required here (so we have`</h1>` to `</h6>`). An example might look like this:

```
<html>
  <head>
    <title>Headings</title>
  </head>
  <body>
    <h1>Storage media</h1>
    At present there is a wide variety of electronic
    storage media. Basically these can be classified
```

```
          as magnetic or
          optical.
          <h2>Magnetic storage media</h2>
          Tapes and diskettes are examples of
          magnetic media.
          <h3>Tapes</h3>
          Tapes are distinguished by their high
          storage capacity. However the disadvantage is
          their relatively slow read and
          write speeds.
          <h3>Diskettes</h3>
          The common type is the 3,5" diskette. These
          can store up to 1.44 MB of data.
          <h2>Optical storage media</h2>
          In this category the CD-ROM and
          more recently the DVD are the most important.
          <h3>CD-ROM</h3>
          A CD-ROM holds up to 700 MB of data.
          <h3>DVD</h3>
          A DVD (digital versatile disk holds up to 18 GB.
        </body>
      </html>
```

Now look at the result of this source code:

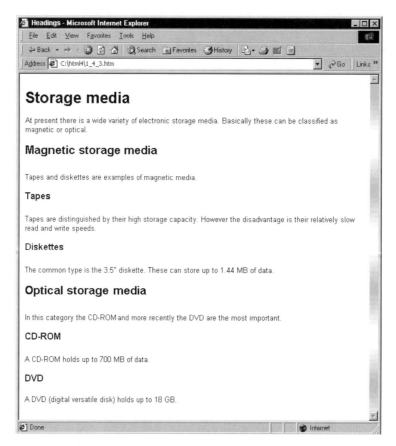

Figure 1.10 *Headings are quite simple to produce*

As you can see a heading closing tag already contains a line break. An additional `<br>` is therefore no longer necessary.

1.4.4 Highlighting passages of text

Sometimes it is useful to highlight words or whole sentences. A number of tags have been created to do this:

→ `<b>` ... `</b>` enable you to output text in bold. This tag you will already be familiar with.

→ Using `<i>` ... `</i>` will display the text in italic.

→ Sometimes you might simply want to use a different font for visual relief. Helpful here is the tag `<tt>` as it can represent text in teletype.

➔ Some browsers can interpret <blink> ... </blink>. A section of text enclosed in this way displays a blinking effect on the screen.

There are many other possibilities but these are very specific and may also be interpreted differently by different browsers. You can find further details on these tags in the quick reference section of the book.

1.4.5 Aligning text

In many cases it is necessary to center a section of text across the page. Helpful here is the pair <center> ... </center>. When you come to use the tags you have just learnt you will be able to create the following source code:

```
<html>
  <head>
    <title>Text formatting</title>
  </head>
  <body>
    As is fairly usual this text is aligned to the left
    side of the window.<br/>
    <center>
      As opposed to this text which is centered.<br/>
    </center>
    You can also show text in <b>bold, <i>bold &amp;
    italic</i></b> or just in <i>italics</i>
    .<br/>
  </body>
</html>
```

Now look at the result in Internet Explorer.

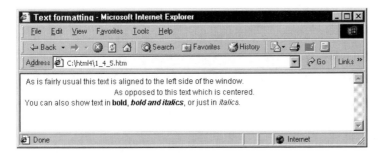

Text formatting - Microsoft Internet Explorer

File Edit View Favorites Tools Help

Back • ➔ • ◎ ⚙ ⌂ | ◎ Search ⚑ Favorites ◈ History | ▤• ⬤ ▣ ▤

Address ⓔ C:\html4\1_4_5.htm   ▼ | ∂ Go | Links »

As is fairly usual this text is aligned to the left side of the window.
                  As opposed to this text which is centered.
You can also show text in **bold**, ***bold and italics***, or just in *italics*.

⬤ Done   ⬤ Internet

Figure 1.11 *Using simple techniques you can highlight important sections of text*

As you can see it's possible to nest highlighting tags as part of the text is output in bold as well as italic at the same time.

1.5 Links

One advantage of HTML pages for normal text is that you can create links to other HTML pages. It was this technique that first made surfing in the www possible.

1.5.1 Internal links

In the case of such links it does not matter whether you want to jump to a page on your own server, on a remote server or maybe even within a page. In this section we'll first of all only concern ourselves with pages on the same computer as the start page.

The following code creates a page which I would ask you to save in C:\HTML4\a.htm.

```
<html>
<head>
<title>Page A</title>
</head>
<body>
<p>You are on page A.</p>
<p>Please click <a href="b.htm">here</a> to go to page B.</
p>
</body>
</html>
```

The source for the page C:\HTML4\b.htm follows.

```
<html>
<head>
<title>Page B</title>
</head>
<body>
<p>You are on page B.</p>
<p>Please click <a href="a.htm">here</a> to go back to page
A.</p>
</body>
</html>
```

Let's look at the page a.htm in the browser:

Figure 1.12 *Links are displayed in a different color and underlined*

Besides the word "here" being displayed in a different color and underlined the change in the mouse pointer also stands out when you move it over this word. So now click on the highlighted spot and you will go to page B where you will find a link back to page A. You can thus jump from page A to page B and back again.

This effect is made possible by the tag `<a>` ... `</a>`. This defines an anchor. It acts as the starting point for the link since the viewer of the HTML page has got to click the page somewhere to initiate the jump to the next page. You must assign to the `href` attribute the file name of the target page.

If instead you refer to another file format on an HTML page (for example an `.exe` or `.zip` file) the browser will also display this if the appropriate subprogram (plug-in) has been installed.

Figure 1.13 *Here the user has the choice of opening the file with an external program or saving to disk*

If the user chooses the save option the browser will ask where the user wants the file stored. The file is then downloaded from the Internet and stored on the user's computer.

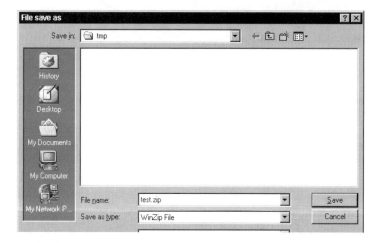

Figure 1.14 *The file is stored straight away ...*

If you have built a directory structure you can use relative pathnames. The browser always searches first in the directory where the initial file is. If for example in the file `C:\HTML4\test\index.htm` you use the link `<a href="start.htm">` this will call the page `C:\HTML4\test\start.htm`. Use `<a href="new/start.htm">` and you will jump to the page `C:\HTML4\test\new\start.htm`. `<a href="../start.htm">` refers to `C:\HTML4\start.htm` and `<a href="../new/start.htm">` would call the file `C:\HTML4\new\start.htm`.

1.5.2   External links

It would be rather boring if the user could only go between his own pages. Therefore you also have the facility to build a link to pages that do not originate from you.

When you go on to publish your pages you will receive an address under which you can be found. In this way every homepage has a unique address. Since you transfer HTML files using the protocol HTTP (hypertext transfer protocol) these addresses always begin with `http://`. Then follows the server name. Most providers call it "www". Now comes the domain name which states who the server is assigned to. In most cases this is the name of the service provider. The domain ends with the country code. Thus `.uk` for example stands for United Kingdom and `.com` for companies that are mostly in the USA. After the country code you can optionally add a directory and a file name. This is not always necessary as there is often a start file which the browser can find automatically. An address could therefore look like:

```
http://www.firm.com/dir/sub_dir/file.htm
```

You can also readily add further subdirectories. Since this address is fictitious you will not find a homepage here, just an error message. We'll now put a real address in the field which you have already used before to dial in your page. What about:

```
http://www.netscape.com/
```

The browser will now build a connection to the network and after a few seconds spent loading, the Netscape homepage will appear. When you want to include such an external link in an HTML page do it this way:

```
Click <a href="http://www.netscape.com/">here</a>

for Netscape.
```

All you need now is a mouse click and you're right there where you want to be.

1.5.3   Telnet

The Internet is not just the world wide web with homepages but also has other services to offer. So it's not enough just to move between pages. A favorite service is the Telnet. There you can dial into a computer and directly execute commands or run programs. This offers the possibility of setting up games which several users can take part in at the same time although they may be sitting at computers in totally different countries. Or you could query online airports about a flight arrival.

Since you also have to use addresses to call up the Telnet service it's fairly easy to create links. Just tell the browser that it's to do with Telnet and no longer the protocol HTTP. The whole thing might then look like this:

```
If you like adventure join in the role-play with

<a href="telnet://epacris.mud.de">EPACRIS</a>.
```

Paste this text into an HTML page in the usual way and via the link EPACRIS you'll be able to take part in the game of the same name. The browser will then start a Telnet program.

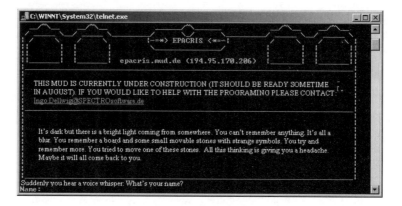

Figure 1.15 *The start screen for EPACRIS in a Telnet window*

However if your browser just outputs an error message saying it cannot find the application you should then insert a Telnet program. In the case of Netscape go to the menu item Options / General Settings / Applications. (Windows 95/98 packages the program in `C:\WINDOWS\TELNET.EXE`.) Microsoft Internet Explorer actually controls this program.

Once the application has opened successfully it builds a connection to the specified address. In this case that will be `epacris.mud.de`. Once the connection exists a short welcome message appears on the screen, you can then choose a name and password and play the game. Of course there are many more addresses to do with quite different topics.

1.5.4 FTP

The term FTP stands for file transfer protocol. This protocol is useful when you want to transfer files. There are providers in the Internet who supply file archives and offer precisely this protocol for file transfers. If for instance you want to access a software company's file list the link might look like this:

```
Here you can look at the latest programs from
<a href="ftp://ftp.microsoft.com">Microsoft</a>.
```

The browser then dials up the given address with guest access and displays the file list.

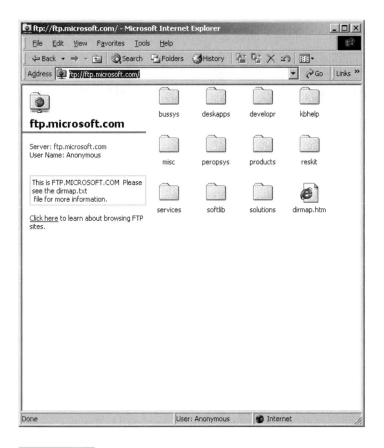

Figure 1.16 *Most browsers have an FTP program built in*

Here you can move through folders as in a file manager and also receive files by simply clicking on them.

1.5.5 E-mail

What would the Internet be without electronic mail? There is an alternative to simply typing your e-mail address into the text. You can in fact create a link to your personal e-mail address like this:

```
Here you can send an
<a href="mailto:Ingo.Dellwig@SPECTROsoftware.de?sub-
ject=Nitty Gritty HTML 4">e-mail</a>
to the author of this book.
```

Warning Unlike other protocols `mailto:` does not use `//`.

Tip The part `?subject=Nitty Gritty HTML 4` can be left out of the address. Its only purpose is to insert a subject directly into the e-mail.

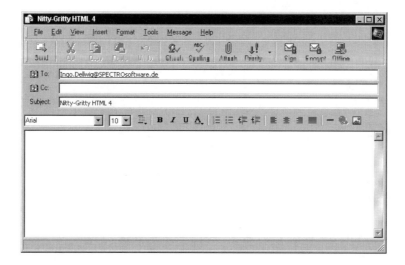

Figure 1.17 *An e-mail window called up by the HTML code and already showing an entry in the subject field as well as the address*

Check it out and let me know if everything has worked out so far.

1.5.6 Jumping within a page

Quite often you want to publish a long list. It's then useful if the user can jump at will to certain places in this list. Hence the tag `<a>` can take the `name` attribute. An alphabetically sorted list could contain this entry:

```
<a name="M">M</a>
```

A list of all the entries beginning with "M" should follow this line. Later on the letter "M" will not appear as a link on the page. So you will not be able to click on it. It serves only as a target point for this link:

```
<a href="#M">
This gets you to the first entry beginning with M.
</a>
```

Clicking on this link brings you to the target point previously defined. This way you can navigate quickly through long pages.

It often happens that you want to produce lists on an HTML page. That can start with hobbies and end up as a product range.

1.6.1   Unordered lists

If you approach this topic as a novice you might produce a list something like this:

```
<html>
  <head>
    <title>A novice list</title>
  </head>
  <body>
    <h1>Internet languages</h1>
    - HTML is the Internet language developed for building
    homepages. It is the
    standard language in the www.<br>
    - CGI scripts are programs that run on
    servers.<br>
    - Java scripts run mostly on the user's computer,
    though there are server side variants.
  </body>
</html>
```

The result of the novice then looks something like this:

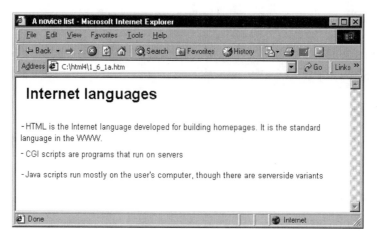

Figure 1.18 *This result does not meet the demands of a professional HTML page*

As you see the text wraps at the end of the line and starts the next line under the list bullet. That does not look very professional.

If we now want to make a list in which every item can consist of several lines of text we can no longer very well begin with a minus as the bullet since we would have to place two spaces before the second line for optimal formatting. A manual count would also be necessary for we would always have to force a line break. How should we otherwise know where to put the spaces? But as every browser may have a different page width this method is in any case a compromise. However HTML has a simple solution. It's called unordered lists.

In the previous example some of the items have several lines. We must therefore first tell the browser that some kind of unordered list now follows. The tag `<ul>` ... `</ul>` does this job. Individual items are bracketed using `<li>` ... `</li>`.

So we can now rewrite the example thus:

```
<html>
  <head>
    <title>A professional list</title>
  </head>
  <body>
    <h1>Internet languages</h1>
    <ul>
      <li>
        HTML is the Internet language developed for building
        homepages. It is the
        standard language in the www.
      </li>
      <li>
        CGI scripts are programs that run on
        servers.
      </li>
      <li>
        JavaScript run mostly on the user's computer,
        though there are server side
        variants.
      </li>
    </ul>
  </body>
</html>
```

The result of the professional variant look like this:

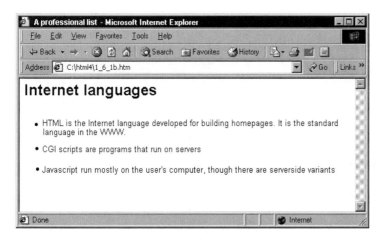

Figure 1.19 *Your list can look as neat as this too*

You can see that all the items in the list appear precisely formatted.

1.6.2   Ordered lists

Assume we now want a list that does not just have the same bullets but we want a list that's numbered. This would then be exactly the right time to use an ordered list. In the following example instead of the `<ul> ... </ul>` tags for an unordered list I have used the tags for an ordered list `<ol> ... </ol>`.

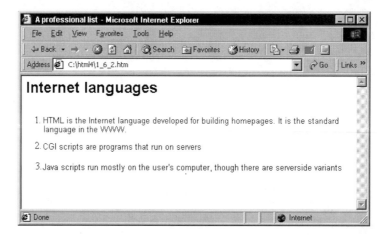

Figure 1.20   *A couple of tweaks is all it takes to turn an unordered into an ordered list*

If you do not want figures many browsers also give you the option of changing the numbering. For this you can use the `type` attribute. This can have the following values:

Value	Result
1	1, 2, 3, 4, 5, 6, ...
A	A, B, C, D, E, F, ...
a	a, b, c, d, e, f, ...
I	I, II, III, IV, V, VI, ...
i	i, ii, iii, iv, v, vi, ...

Table 1.2 *Various ways of numbering a list*

But sometimes you may not want to begin your list with the number one but say the number nine. This is where the `start` attribute helps. Using these two new attributes you could then create the following HTML text:

```
<html>
  <head>
    <title>Roman numerals</title>
  </head>
  <body>
    <ol type="I" start="9">
      <li>Number 9</li>
      <li>Number 10</li>
      <li>Number 11</li>
    </ol>
  </body>
</html>
```

Here then is how the numbers nine to eleven look in Roman number format.

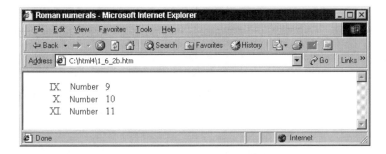

Figure 1.21 *The browser even knows the Roman number format*

As you can see it is actually possible to use several attributes in a tag.

1.7 Tables

When you want to give text a special format or present a lot of figures clearly then you can't get around using tables.

1.7.1 Basic structure of a table

One great advantage of HTML is that you can create tables quite easily. For instance if you want to convey several lines of data to the visitor to the page you should make this as clear as possible. The complete table code is enclosed by `<table> ... </table>`. A table is a relatively complex entity whose appearance you can influence by a number of attributes.

→ The border attribute for instance specifies the width of the table border. If you use a "0" here the table will not have a border. For new browsers the default value for border is "0".

→ Use cellpadding to specify how many pixels you want between the table text and the cell border.

→ cellspacing specifies on the other hand the separation between the cells themselves.

→ In addition you can use width to specify the overall width of the table you want. Here you can enter an absolute value in pixels or a percentage of the width of the screen.

→ Of course you can also set the height. Use it like width but you must use the height attribute.

Here are a couple of examples:

```
<table>
```

A table beginning like this has no border. The text would just be formatted as in a table. There would not even be any lines separating the individual elements.

```
<table border=1 cellpadding=5 width=100>
```

This table has a border of minimum width. The overall distance of the text from the gridlines is five pixels and the table is overall exactly 100 pixels wide.

```
<table border=10 cellpadding=10 width=50%>
```

This table gets a wide border. Each cell is 10 pixels from the next. The entire table takes up half the width of the browser.

1.7.2 Entering data

Although we can now specify what the table looks like how does the data actually get into the table? Since we write from left to right and from top to bottom it also makes sense to proceed line by line when creating a table. Enclose each line in a table using `<tr> ... </tr>` (table row). Each line has several entries so tag these using `<td> ... </td>` (table data). If you want a cell element to contain a table header use `<th> ... </th>` (table header) instead. A table might therefore look like:

```
<html>
  <head>
    <title>Browser statistics</title>
  </head>
  <body>
    <table border=1>
      <tr>
```

```
      <th>Browser</th>
      <th>Market share</th>
    </tr>
    <tr>
      <td>Microsoft Internet Explorer</td>
      <td>60.4 %</td>
    </tr>
    <tr>
      <td>Netscape Communicator</td>
      <td>38.5 %</td>
    </tr>
    <tr>
      <td>Other</td>
      <td>1.1 %</td>
    </tr>
    </table>
  </body>
</html>
```

The result already looks pretty good but I promise you there are still a few things we can improve on.

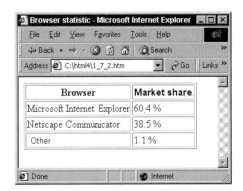

Figure 1.22 *A table makes the data look much clearer*

1.7.3 Formatting tables

Now we'll give the table a further line to show its status. If we enter text simply into a single cell this would just be the size of a single column. However it looks more professional if the comment runs across both columns. There is an attribute specifically for this. Use `colspan` to specify the number of columns you want a cell to span. Insert this attribute then in the tag `<td>` or even `<th>`. We could therefore extend the table with the following lines:

```
<tr>
  <td colspan=2>Status: July 2000</td>
</tr>
```

You can also see that you can skip cells simply by leaving out text. Since it's possible to span several columns an element can of course also span several rows. In this case use the `rowspan` attribute.

There's one thing I haven't yet mentioned though. By now you will have realized that the width of columns is calculated according to the text they contain. However you'll often need a table with columns of equal width. That's why you can specify the width of individual columns. The simplest way is to define the `width` attribute, which we've already used for the overall table width, in each cell in the first table row. That way you can fix the width for all columns. You could equally use the attribute `height` in the first cell of a row to fix its height.

1.7.4 Aligning text in tables

So far we've always written text left-aligned. That doesn't look very professional with figures. So how can we right-align or center table text? You could of course use `<center>` in every table cell to center the text along the horizontal axis. But there's an easier way! You can define the `align` attribute for an entire table row as well as for individual cells. It can take the following values:

Value	Effect
left	Aligns the text to the left.
center	Centers the text.
right	Aligns the text to the left.

Table 1.3 *Values of the align attribute in tables*

For alignment along the vertical axis `valign` is the attribute to use. You can use it with these values:

Value	Effect
top	Aligns the text to the top edge of the cell.
middle	Centers the text vertically.
bottom	Aligns the text to the bottom edge of the cell.

Table 1.4 *Values of the valign attribute in tables*

Let's just check out this new knowledge:

```html
<html>
<head>
    <title>Cell alignment</title>
  </head>
  <body>
    <table border=1>
      <tr valign="top">
        <td width=100 height=100 align="left">
        top-left</td>
        <td width=100 height=100 align="center">
        top-center</td>
        <td width=100 height=100 align="right">
        top-right</td>
      </tr>
      <tr valign="middle">
        <td width=100 height=100 align="left">
        middle-left</td>
        <td width=100 height=100 align="center">
        middle-center</td>
        <td width=100 height=100 align="right">
        middle-right</td>
      </tr>
      <tr valign="bottom">
        <td width=100 height=100 align="left">
        bottom-left</td>
        <td width=100 height=100 align="center">
        bottom-center</td>
        <td width=100 height=100 align="right">
        bottom-right</td>
      </tr>
    </table>
  </body>
</html>
```

The result is in the browser:

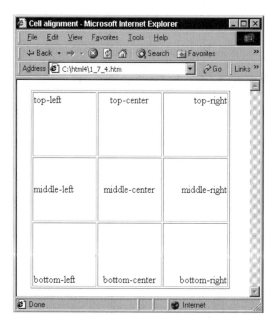

START UP!

Figure 1.23 *Here you can easily see how to align text in a table*

1.8 Typeface

In Chapter 2 we shall meet some ways for highlighting text passages. Sometimes though it isn't enough to write everything in the same font size and in the same font style. That's why there are some further useful options for modifying the typeface.

1.8.1   Font size

Of course you've got to be able to somehow identify the sections of text where you want the typeface to look different. For this you use `<font> ... </font>`. One of the attributes you can assign to this tag is `size`, which can take values from 1 to 7. Simply typing in a number will output the text in this font size. If you don't always want to check what size is actually being used but you nevertheless need a smaller font size you can also set a sign.

```
<font size=-2>
```

This tag would therefore produce a font two sizes smaller than that previously used. If you need a larger font you can of course also go the other way. For example:

```
<font size=+3>
```

To avoid having to enclose the entire body of your page with `<font>` ... `</font>` you can also just set a standard font at the beginning using `<basefont>`. A small example might therefore look like this:

```
<html>
  <head>
    <title>Font sizes</title>
  </head>
  <body><basefont size=3>
    This is now the standard font.<br>
    <font size=-3>0</font>
    <font size=-2>1</font>
    <font size=-1>2</font>
    <font size=+0>3</font>
    <font size=+1>4</font>
    <font size=+2>5</font>
    <font size=+3>6</font>
    <font size=+4>7</font>
    <font size=+5>8</font>
  </body>
</html>
```

We can tell quite a bit from a quick look at the result:

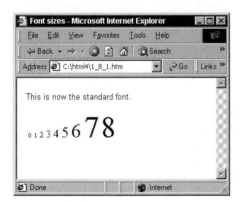

Figure 1.24 *The font size can be changed in seven steps*

Here we can see that really only the values one to seven are meaningful as zero and one match each other for size as do the figures seven and eight.

1.8.2   Fonts

Another attribute that can considerably improve the appearance of a page is face.

```
<font face="arial">
```

A section of text starting with this will be displayed in the font "arial". This must of course be installed on the visitor's computer. This is why you can also specify several fonts since the browser will then search through these in sequence. The comma acts here as a separator.

```
<font face="any font, igloolaser, arial">Test</font>
```

In this example you can easily see how to handle different fonts. The browser first tries to display the word "Test" in the font "any font". If this is not installed it searches for IglooLaser. Only then does it switch to "arial".

1.9 Colors

Somehow everything we've designed so far has been rather colorless. It's high time that we brought some color into play. First of all we ought to look at how a computer displays colors.

1.9.1   How are colors produced?

We can split a color into three primary colors. Since the monitor emits light we are concerned here with the primary colors of the additive color mixture . These are red, green and blue. If for example we directed a red, a green and a blue lamp onto a point the light arriving would be white. If we could now individually adjust the brightness of the lamps we could produce almost any color. This means we can uniquely define a color based on the brightness of the red, green and blue components. We talk here of the RGB coding. Each color component can have a value between 0 and 255. We type this number in the hexadecimal notation which is a system based on sixteen numbers. All the values between 00 and FF are possible. In case you've never worked in this system I've listed these numbers for your information in Appendix C.

So that you get a rough idea how each color is represented I have summarized the most important ones here:

Color	RGB coding
Black	00 00 00
White	FF FF FF
Red	FF 00 00
Lime	00 FF 00
Blue	00 00 FF
Yellow	FF FF 00
Brown	99 66 33
Cyan	00 FF FF
Fuchsia	FF 00 FF
Purple	80 00 80
Maroon	80 00 00
Green	00 80 00
Navy	00 00 80
Silver	C0 C0 C0
Gray	A0 A0 A0
Dark gray	80 80 80

Table 1.5 *The most important colors and their coding*

You will find a more complete table in Appendix B.

1.9.2 Changing text colors

We've already met `<font>` in the last section. Now you have another attribute called `color`. With this we can define the text color. Some browsers actually only support RGB coding, so you should specify the color in this form too.

```
<font color="#FFFF00">
```

This tag you would therefore place before text you want displayed in yellow. Please note that there must be a hash sign (#) before the values of each color so that the browser can recognize the need for RGB coding. New browsers however also understand explicit color names. So you can achieve the same thing with:

```
<font color="yellow">
```

Please refer to the names and their RGB coding in the table in Appendix B.

You will have certainly noticed by now that links have their own particular color. You can also set this color yourself in the `<body>`. You just declare the desired color to the `link` attribute. You can also assign a color to the `vlink` attribute.

This is for links already visited. You can also assign a color to `alink`. This is for links pointing to the current page. Another attribute is `text`. You can assign it the color for normal text.

```
<body text=" #FFFFFF" link=" #00FF00" vlink=" #FF0000"
alink=" #0000FF" >
```

A body beginning like this will show normal text in white, links in green, visited links in red and links to the same page in blue.

1.9.3   Background color

If you don't like the gray or white background simply choose another color. Once again define this in the `<body>` tag but you must assign it to the `bgcolor` attribute.

```
<body bgcolor="#FFBBBB">
```

This page will get a background in the color pink. You can even define the background for individual table cells by inserting the `bgcolor` attribute in the tag `<td>` for the table content. So use this to create a table showing the most important colors and their RGB coding. The source code for this table might then look like this:

```
<html>
  <head>
    <title>Color table</title>
  </head>
  <body>
    <table border=5>
      <tr>
        <td bgcolor="#FFFFFF"><font color="#000000">
          Black</font><td>00 00 00
        <td bgcolor="#000000"><font color="#FF00FF">
          Fuchsia</font><td>FF 00 FF
      <tr>
        <td bgcolor="#000000"><font color="#FFFFFF">
          White</font><td>FF FF FF
        <td bgcolor="#FFFFFF"><font color="#800080">
          Purple</font><td>80 00 80
      <tr>
        <td bgcolor="#000000"><font color="#FF0000">
          Red</font><td>FF 00 00
        <td bgcolor="#FFFFFF"><font color="#800000">
          Maroon</font><td>80 00 00
```

```
    <tr>
      <td bgcolor="#000000"><font color="#00FF00">
        Lime</font><td>00 FF 00
      <td bgcolor="#FFFFFF"><font color="#008000">
        Green</font><td>00 80 00
    <tr>
      <td bgcolor="#000000"><font color="#0000FF">
        Blue</font><td>00 00 FF
      <td bgcolor="#FFFFFF"><font color="#000080">
        Navy</font><td>00 00 80
    <tr>
      <td bgcolor="#000000"><font color="#FFFF00">
        Yellow</font><td>FF FF 00
      <td bgcolor="#000000"><font color="#C0C0C0">
        Silver</font><td>C0 C0 C0
    <tr>
      <td bgcolor="#000000"><font color="#996633">
        Brown</font><td>99 66 33
      <td bgcolor="#000000"><font color="#A0A0A0">
        Gray</font><td>A0 A0 A0
    <tr>
      <td bgcolor="#000000"><font color="#00FFFF">
        Cyan</font><td>00 FF FF
      <td bgcolor="#000000"><font color="#808080">
        Dark gray</font><td>80 80 80
    </table>
  </body>
</htm>
```

The result shows the most common colors on the screen:

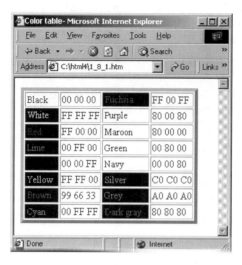

Figure 1.25 *The most important colors and their RGB codings*

Unfortunately we can only show the colors here in shades of gray but if you look at the example with a browser they'll show their full effect.

1.10 Graphics

Current browsers will display not just text but also graphics. Use these to liven up your homepage and give it a professional touch. The possibilities are almost endless.

1.10.1 Displaying graphics

All the common browsers can display images in the formats `.gif` and `.jpg` or `.jpeg`. Before adding an image to a page you should if at all possible convert it to one of these formats if you've not already done so. One way to do this is to load a graphic into a drawing program and simply re-save it in one of the two formats.

Tip So after uploading take another look at your page via an Internet connection and decide if the page loads fast enough.

You should also watch that the graphic is not too big as it always takes rather longer over the Internet to load all the images.

If you now want to add a graphic to a page you'll have to use `<img>`. Give the `src` attribute in the tag the name of the graphic. That might then look like:

```
<img src="an_image.gif">
```

If you want to add an image that resides somewhere on a totally different computer you can also type in a complete address:

```
<IMG src="http://www.firm.com/directory/an_image.gif">
```

The `alt` attribute of the `img` element can be used to place text information about a picture, which is displayed before the picture downloads, or if the picture fails to download, or if the user has switched off the displaying of pictures (which some do). It is also very useful from the point of view of searchability - you can search through a HTML file for information that might be held in `alt` tags, that you can't very well do with a picture only.

```
<img src="an_image.gif" alt="image">
```

A modern browser would display the graphic `an_image.gif` here. But an older browser that can't display images would only output the word "image". New browsers display the text of the `alt` attribute if you put the mouse over the image and don't move it for about two seconds. This is the way then to add information to images and graphics that are not immediately visible but can nevertheless be retrieved. This makes sense if for example text would spoil the graphical design.

1.10.2 Aligning graphics

In many cases we want to add an image to a page yet still show text right next to it. It's advisable here to fix the alignment of the text to the image. The `align` attribute for the `<img>` tag does this job. It can take three values:

Value	Effect
top	The text is aligned to the top of the image.
middle	The text is aligned to the middle of the image.
bottom	The text is aligned to the bottom of the image.

Table 1.6 *Values of the align attribute for images*

You can see that it's not the image to the text that's aligned but the text to the image. As a demonstration of the `align` attribute display the following page:

```
<html>
  <head>
```

```
    <title>Text to image alignment</title>
  </head>
  <body>
    <img src="an_image.gif" align="top">
    Text aligned to top of image.<br/>
    <img src="an_image.gif" align="middle">
    Text aligned to middle of image.<br/>
    <img src="an_image.gif" align="bottom">
    Text aligned to bottom of image.<br/>
  </body>
</html>
```

The page looks like this:

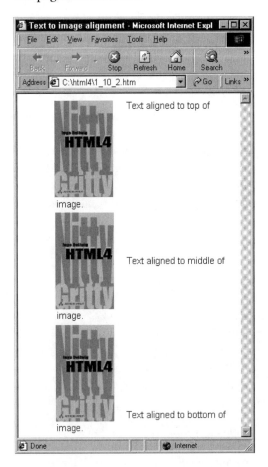

Figure 1.26 *The various alignments of text to a graphic*

If you put text next to an image that projects beyond the edge of the browser window there's a problem. The text no longer fits in next to the image but continues below the line break. I therefore recommend putting the images and text in a table since you can align these much more precisely and the text stays in its cell.

If the image appears too big or too small you can modify its height and width with the `height` and `width` attributes in the `<img>` tag. As usual you can directly type in the number of pixels or the percentage screen width or height. If you're only using one of the attributes the image will adjust to the size change in the other direction.

```html
<html>
  <head>
    <title>Different image sizes </title>
  </head>
  <body>
    <img src="an_image.gif" width=100% height=50><p>
    <img src="an_image.gif" width=10% height=20%><p>
    <img src="an_image.gif" height=20%><p>
  </body>
</html>
```

Let's take a look at the result in the browser:

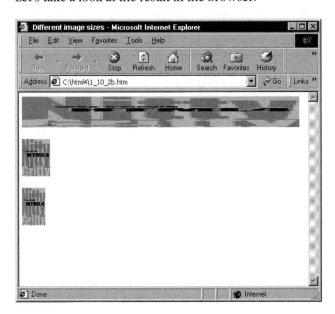

Figure 1.27 *You can set an exact image size*

1.10.3 Using graphics as anchors for links

You can of course also enclose graphics using <a> ... </a>. The link you've created then refers to the image.

```
<a href="http://www.addison-wesley.com">
  <img src="an_imag.gif">
</a>
```

As usual this example will display the image. Click on it and you'll arrive at the Addison Wesley homepage. The image has a colored border indicating the definition of a link. It has the same color as the other links on the page. If this border worries you then turn it off with the attribute border attribute. It's used in <img>. Assign it the value zero to make it disappear.

Tip By the way, you can achieve particularly nice effects with animated .gif files. However this topic is not part of an HTML course but belongs more in a book on web publishing.

1.10.4 Background graphics

You can already change the background color. In many cases though this is not enough. A patterned or textured background is then the solution:

```
<html>
  <head>
    <title> Background </title>
  </head>
  <body background="a_bg.jpg">
    <h1> The graphic fills the background.
    </h1>
  </body>
</html>
```

As you see you can assign the filename of the graphic you want to display directly to the background attribute in the <body> tag.

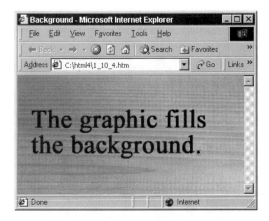

Figure 1.28 *Enhance the browser background with a graphic*

Please avoid if at all possible text colors which occur in the background graphic otherwise it can be difficult to read what's written on your HTML page. In the case of bright text colors also take care to use a background color that is as dark as possible and vice versa.

If you show a little more text on your page or reduce the size of the browser until a scrollbar appears on the right side you can move the image up and down. You'll see that the background always moves along with it. But you can stop that too:

Insert in the `<body>` tag the `bgproperties` attribute with the value `fixed`. This then looks like:

```
<body background="a_bg.jpg" bgproperties="fixed">
```

When scrolling you'll now see that the background remains stationary with just the text running over it like a transparent overlay.

1.10.5   Videos

In exactly the same way you put graphics into documents, with the new browsers you can also play entire videos. Of course you should carefully consider beforehand how big the whole video might be since you can't play it till it's been loaded. That means the visitor might have to wait quite a while before enjoying your video. Many Internet users though have limited patience and will abort the process early.

A video is often in the `.avi` format. You can also use `<img>` to include a video file. The `src` attribute we already know. If possible it should always contain the filename of the start image so any browser that can't run videos will then display this image unless it's actually a pure text browser. For such cases you can always still add the `alt` attribute along with a text description. The video file you then simply assign to the `dynsrc` attribute. I shall assume you've got a film called `a_film.avi` and another file `a_film.jpg` containing the start image of the film. Now test the following HTML page:

```
<html>
  <head>
    <title>A Video</title>
  </head>
  <body>
    <center>
      <h1>A video follows...</h1>
      <img src="a_film.jpg" alt="A film should play
      here." dynsrc="a_film.avi">
    </center>
  </body>
</html>
```

For videos you can also use the `height` and `width` attributes. They are employed in the usual way.

As you've already seen the user can't control the video if you insert it as in the previous example. But if you'd like to give the visitor this option then include the `controls` attribute. It's sufficient to put this attribute in `<img>`. You don't need to assign a value.

```
<img src="a_film.jpg" alt=" A film should play here"
dynsrc="a_film.avi" controls>
```

Now the visitor can use the appropriate buttons to control the running of the video. If you could look at the example using a video-compliant browser you'll have realized that the film runs through once and then stops. But if you want a replay you can specify this directly. The `loop` attribute fulfils this option.

```
<img src="a_film.jpg" alt="A film should play here."
dynsrc="a_film.avi" loop=3>
```

This video would therefore repeat twice after the first play. But with `loop=-1` you can also produce continuous play. With `loopdelay` you have the option of forcing a delay between the plays. Specify this in milliseconds.

```
<img src="a_film.jpg" alt="A film should play here."
dynsrc="a_film.avi" controls loop=-1 loopdelay=3000>
```

This example then would insert a video that plays continuously with a delay of three seconds between plays. Finally you have the option of specifying how the video should start. The attribute for this is simply `start`. It can take two values:

Value	Effect
fileopen	The video starts after the entire page has loaded.
mouseover	Here the film doesn't run until the user moves the mouse pointer into the video window.

Table 1.7 *Values of the start attribute for videos*

1.11   Music and sounds

So far we've concerned ourselves a lot with the look of HTML pages. The aspect of audio design has had rather less than it's fair share. We'll put that right now:

1.11.1   Adding music

If you want to provide your homepage with music, some browsers let you add background music directly. Do it using the `<bgsound>` tag. Place the `src` attribute inside to give the file you want played. A music file might be called `a_song.mid`. This is a typical music file in MIDI format (`.mid`). Adding it to an HTML page then looks like this:

```
<html>
  <head>
    <title>Music</title>
  </head>
  <body>
    <bgsound src="a_song.mid">
    Here's some music!
  </body>
</html>
```

You hear the song once and then it's quiet again. You can of course (as with videos) use the `loop` and `loopdelay` attributes.

```
<bgsound src="a_song.mid" loop=-1 loopdelay=1000>
```

In this example the music plays repeatedly. Between each play there is a pause of one second.

1.11.2   Adding sounds

If you can connect a microphone to your computer you can record sounds or your voice. Do this by creating wave files. They have the file extension `.wav` and you can include them in a homepage with a little trick. Simply insert a link to this

START UP!

file and the browser will play it upon download. The user must click the link first though.

A more user-friendly alternative is to embed auxiliary programs to play these files. To do this use `<embed>` which you can employ as the following example shows:

```html
<html>
  <head>
    <title>Sounds</title>
  </head>
  <body>
    Here's a sound.<br/>
    <embed src="a_sound.wav" autostart=true hidden=true>
  </body>
</html>
```

The `hidden` attribute can take the values `false` or `true`. When you specify you want the auxiliary program hidden with `hidden=true` it doesn't appear on the screen. With Internet Explorer however the place that would be needed for the application is left blank. `autostart` can also take both these values and indicates whether the application will start immediately or the user must first select it.

There's a large number of file types you can embed using this command. For instance, you could also play music and videos in Netscape. If you want your homepage to play music for both Netscape and Internet Explorer you can use a JavaScript that you'll find in the "Tips and tricks" section.

1.12 Frames

So far it's only ever been possible to display one page after the other. But it would be much more convenient if we could show several pages at the same time and move them independently. Frames have been created to do this job.

1.12.1 Dividing a page into frames

If you want to divide up a page into two frames you'll have to create a total of three files. The first defines the size and special features of both frames. We call this page the frameset. The other two will then be loaded into the corresponding sections of the frameset. They are concerned with the content of the frames.

We'll first of all consider the file for building the frame. An HTML file of this sort has the standard head but needn't have a body. Instead insert `<frameset> ... </frameset>`. It tells the browser that frame definitions follow.

Since you can divide a page horizontally or vertically type one of the following attributes in this tag. You've got `cols` or `rows`. These define the columns (horizontally separated frames) and rows (vertically separated frames) respectively.

```
<frameset cols=20%,80%>
```

This would divide the page into two columns: the left column taking 20% of the browser window width and the right one the remaining 80%. Or directly type in the number of pixels like before. Another way is to enter the relative data using a special syntax:

```
<frameset rows=40,2*,*>
```

This example would create three rows. The top row would be exactly 40 pixels high. The two lower ones divide the rest of the screen in the ratio 2:1.

Each row or column must now have a link to an HTML page otherwise there would be no content displayed. That's why for each frame you insert the `<frame>` tag. Using the `src` attribute you can now type in the file that you want to appear in the frame.

In case everything still isn't clear I'd like to illustrate the options that frames offer with a few examples. First of all we'll need some files to display in the frames. So now create the six pages `a.htm` to `f.htm` which all display just a single letter. The first would therefore look like:

```
<html>
  <head>
    <title>A</title>
  </head>
  <body>
  A
  </body>
</html>
```

For the following five files you can simply replace both instances of the letter A by B through F.

Now we still need a page to create the frames. We'll simply call them `frame.htm`:

```
<html>
  <head>
    <title>Example of Frames</title>
  </head>
  <frameset rows=20%,60%,20%>
    <frame src="a.htm">
    <frameset cols=50%,50%>
      <frame src="b.htm">
```

```
        <frame src="c.htm">
      </frameset>
      <frame src="d.htm">
    </frameset>
  </html>
```

Let's look at the browser display:

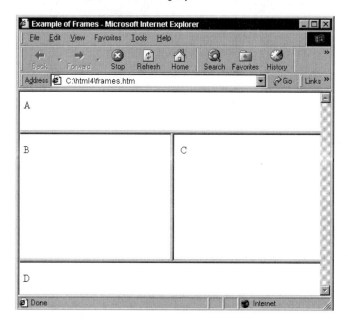

Figure 1.29
The definition of frames allows several pages to be displayed at the same time

If you now look at this file you'll see that you can also use a `<frameset>` tag inside a subordinate frame definition. Do this to subdivide an existing frame into several sections.

You can adjust the borders of individual frames in this example as desired by dragging them with the mouse. If you don't want to give the site visitor this option you can insert into `<frame>` the attribute " `noresize`".

Surely you have already noticed that the browser normally always leaves a narrow margin at the sides, top and bottom. But if you now want to place a graphic or text close to the frame border you need further attributes. That will be necessary, for example, if you want a frame that is relatively small and completely filled with a graphic. The `marginheight` attribute therefore determines the size of the top and bottom margins. Use `marginwidth` to also define the side margins.

These attributes expect the number of pixels that you want to specify for the margins. However they must be greater than zero. The value one is therefore the smallest possible frame width.

It may of course be that the size of a frame is not sufficient to show all the information in it. That occurs for example if the frame is too small, the resolution too low or the content is simply too much. Of course there's a solution to this: scrollbars. A browser can also create these for your frames if required. The `scrolling` attribute can now define how you want the browser to behave in relation to these scrollbars. For this attribute there are three different values:

Value	Effect
auto	A scrollbar is added if required.
yes	A scrollbar is always displayed.
no	A scrollbar is never added even if required.

Table 1.8 *Values of the scrolling attribute for frames*

1.12.2   Targeting frames

As there are now several pages on the screen at the same time all possibly with links, you must bear in mind a couple of things about links in a frame-compliant page.

How can the browser know in which frame to build the page the link refers to? There's one simple rule it will definitely always obey: unless otherwise set by default a new page is always built in the frame where the link is activated. So if in page a.htm you now add the following link inside the body, the browser will display the file e.htm in the frame where the page a.htm previously was.

```
<html>
  <head>
    <title>A</title>
  </head>
  <body>
  A<br>
  <a href="e.htm">To page E.</a><br>
  </body>
</html>
```

In many cases though we'd like to open a page in another frame. So we give each `<frame>` tag a name. The `name` attribute does this. You could therefore easily change the file frame.htm in the following manner:

```
<html>
  <head>
```

```
       <title> Example of frames</title>
     </head>
     <frameset rows=20%,60%,20%>
       <frame src="a.htm" name="top">
       <frameset cols=50%,50%>
         <frame src="b.htm" name="middle left">
         <frame src="c.htm" name="middle right">
       </frameset>
       <frame src="d.htm" name="bottom">
     </frameset>
</html>
```

Once we've named the frames we can give each link a target frame. For tag `<a>` then there's the further attribute `target` which contains the name of the frame we want to display the next page in. So in the body of a.htm add the following line:

```
<a href="f.htm" target="bottom">Page F (bottom)</a>
```

If you now select this link the page f.htm will appear in the lower frame.

For the `target` attribute there are four predefined values which assign the next page to a quite special target.

Value	Effect
_SELF	Loads the next page into the same frame.
_PARENT	Updates the frame.
_BLANK	Shows the next page in a new browser window.
_TOP	Loads the page at the top frame level.

Table 1.9 *Values for the TARGET attribute for frames*

If you're using one particular target for most of the links on a page it makes a lot of sense to make use of `<base>`. This tag actually allows you to set a standard target frame.

```
<base target="bottom">
```

This command means that all links without their own `target` attribute will appear directly in the frame called `bottom`.

1.12.3   Browsers without frame support

Frames only came in with the more recent versions of Netscape Navigator and Microsoft Internet Explorer. So there are still some older browsers that don't support frames. If such a browser were to hit a framed site it would not be able to interpret `<frame>` and would only show an empty screen. That's why in all frame-compliant browsers there is a further tag specifying an area to write HTML text in so that old browsers can display it. It's called `<noframes>` and is used as in the following example:

```html
<html>
  <head>
    <title> Example of frames</title>
  </head>
  <frameset rows=20%,60%,20%>
    <frame src="a.htm" name="top">
    <frameset cols=50%,50%>
      <frame src="b.htm" name="middle left">
      <frame src="c.htm" name="middle right">
    </frameset>
    <frame src="d.htm" name="bottom">
  </frameset>
  <noframes>
    <head>
      <title>Example of frames (sorry your browser is too
      old)</title>
    </head>
    <body>
      <center>
        WARNING!<p>
        YOU ARE USING A BROWSER THAT DOES NOT SUPPORT
        FRAMES.  CLICK
        <a href="a.htm">HERE</a> FOR A VERSION WITH NO
        FRAMES.<p>
      </center>
    </body>
  </noframes>
</html>
```

This browser does not support frames and displays the `noframes` section:

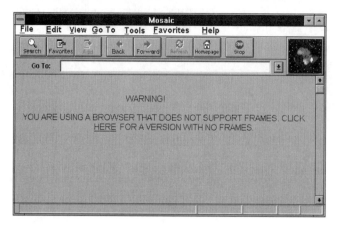

Figure 1.30 *Even though there are few users still around with such old browsers it's advisable to produce a special message for these*

A user with an old browser therefore sees the message entered in the `<nofra-mes>` ... `</noframes>` area. Here it's quite easy to insert a link to a page without a frame.

1.13 Forms

A homepage is always an information source for the visitor to the site. Sometimes though we want to get information from this person. In many cases it will do to give the e-mail address and ask the visitor to our site to write us an e-mail. But if we always need the same type of information and want to make it as easy as possible for the user then forms are a worthwhile alternative.

1.13.1 Text fields

Let's assume you'd like to ask for a surfer's address. Then this method wouldn't be very professional:

```
<html>
  <head>
    <title>Address</title>
  </head>
  <body>
    If you'd like to get in touch with me
    just write me an
```

```
    <a href="mailto:my@address.com">e-mail</a> with your
    address, e-mail address, phone and fax numbers.
  </body>
</html>
```

This example is certainly not very convenient since the site visitor must keep everything he has to write in the mail. It might be much better here to create a form.

A form like this is identified by `<form>` ... `</form>`. There are two important attributes that you should always assign to `<form>`. The first is called `method`. I'll mention here just for the sake of completeness what it does: `method` specifies how you want the data sent.

Value	Effect
post	Here the data are sent as a separate data stream direct to the script.
get	Here the data are attached to the URL and then passed together with it to the target script.

Table 1.10 *Values of the method attribute in forms*

Actually for us only the `post` value is important.

The second attribute that you should always specify is `action` and specifies the address of the script. As scripts are not dealt with in this book you only need know that you can also give an e-mail address for sending the content of forms to. A form tag might therefore look like:

```
<form method="post" action="mailto:my@address.com">
```

This sends an e-mail along with the content of the form to the address `my@address.com`.

To start with we define an input field that may have several lines of text. For this use `<textarea>` ... `</textarea>`. So you can assign each form element a value later on, every element has a name. So the `name` attribute is defined for `<textarea>`. Now the browser only has to know how big the text field is to be. That's why we specify the `rows` and `cols` attributes.

```
<textarea name="comments" rows=3 cols=40>
This is the default text in the field.
It needs no <br> tags.
</textarea>
```

This text field is called "comments" and it has three rows with 40 columns. The text between the opening and closing tag is placed directly into the new text field. The address request might then look like this:

```
<html>
  <head>
    <title>Address</title>
  </head>
  <body>
    If you'd like to get in touch with me
    just write me an
    <a href="mailto:my@address.com">e-mail</a> with your
    address, e-mail address, phone and fax numbers.

    <form method="post" action="mailto:my@address.com">
      <textarea name="comments" rows=3 cols=40>
      </textarea>
    </form>
  </body>
</html>
```

All data would now be assigned directly to the name "comments". In a form though it most often makes more sense to ask for the different data items separately. For instance you can capture the last and first names separately from the rest. As these are single lines of text a new tag will be needed for each one. Using the <input> tag you can create a good many form elements. So that the browser now knows exactly what's being asked for <input> always has the type attribute. To enable text input type must have the value text. You can determine the width of the text field with the attribute size and the maximum length of text in it with maxlength. If you want to you can even pass a default value to the text input. You'll have to give this value to the attribute value.

```
<input name="LastName" type="text" size=40 maxlength=80
value="Bloggs">
```

This command creates an input field called "LastName" that has width 40 and allows 80 characters as input. When the page is built the name "Bloggs" is already entered.

```
<html>
  <head>
    <title>Address</title>
  </head>
  <body>
    If you'd like to get in touch with me
```

```
just write me an
<a href="mailto:my@address.com">e-mail</a> with your
address, e-mail address, phone and fax numbers.
<form method="post" action="mailto:my@address.com">
  Last name:
  <input name="LastName" type="text" size=40
  maxlength=80 value="Bloggs"><br>
  First name:
  <input name="FirstName" type="text" size=40
  maxlength=80 value="Joe"><br>
  Address:
  <textarea name="Address" rows=3 cols=40>
  </textarea>
</form>
</body>
</html>
```

However it's a long time since a text field was all you could create with a form. There are some important elements still missing.

1.13.2 Radio and check buttons

From your operating system you'll surely know how radio and check buttons work. Nevertheless I'd like to briefly explain here how these buttons differ in their operation.

We often use check buttons when we can choose several options from a list. You'll surely know this process from driving license forms.

Figure 1.31 *You can select more than one check button*

Radio buttons are used in a similar way to select elements from a list. But here you can only select one element. It's a good way to represent a decision between Yes and No.

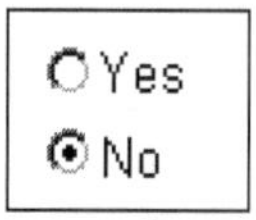

◯ Yes
◉ No

Figure 1.32 *A typical Yes/No request*

If, for example, we want to represent a request for a person's title using radio buttons then in the `<input>` tag we'll now have to set the attribute `type` to the value `radio`. So that the browser knows which radio buttons go together all buttons concerning the same selection must have the same name. The button values set for the `value` attribute will be assigned later to the name of the selection when the corresponding button is selected. You can place the `checked` attribute in the tag of the default button.

```
<input type="radio" name="title" value="Mr." "checked"/>Mr.
<input type="radio" name="title" value="Ms">Ms
```

Here we've designed a decision request named "title" with "Mr." as the default option.

Check buttons are not much different from radio buttons as regards programming. We just pass the `checkbox` value to the `type` attribute. Always use the same name for a selection if at all possible. The individual values are passed using `value` and use the `checked` attribute to make a check button a default choice.

```
<input type="checkbox" name="browser" value="MS
IE">Microsoft Internet Explorer<br>
<input type="checkbox" name="browser"
value="Netscape">Netscape<br>
<input type="checkbox" name="browser"
value="other">Other<br>
```

This is how a request for the browsers a visitor uses most often might look. Several options can be checked.

1.13.3   Drop-down lists

Another way of getting predefined answers is drop-down lists.

Figure 1.33 *You can also create a drop-down list like this with HTML*

For this type of list we have `<select>` ... `</select>`. Assign the names to the list as normal using the `name` attribute. You should also define the number of entries you want displayed simultaneously using `size`. The individual menu items have the `<option>` tag.

```
<select name="Country" size=1>
  <option>USA</option>
  <option>UK</option>
  <option>Germany</option>
  <option>Other</option>
</select>
```

This source text reproduces exactly the menu selection we discussed above. By giving the `size` attribute a value greater than one a number of options become visible at the same time. We can even set `multiple` as an attribute to allow for the selection of several options.

1.13.4   Sending and deleting forms

So now our form is almost ready. The only thing still missing is the facility to send or if necessary delete it. Therefore we'll add two more buttons which we always program as follows:

```
<input type="submit" value="Send form">

<input type="reset" value="Delete form">
```

Send form	Delete form

Figure 1.34 *The left button at least is essential in a form*

So for the `type` attribute use the value `submit` to create a button for sending the form. To delete the form create a button using the `reset` value for the `type` attribute. The `value` attribute always stands for the button label.

The complete address form then looks like this:

```
<html>
  <head>
    <title>Address</title>
  </head>
  <body>
    <form method="post" action="mailto:my@address.com">
      <input type="radio" name="title" value="Mr."
      checked>Mr.
      <input type="radio" name="title"
      value="Ms">Ms<br>
      Last name:
      <input name="LastName" type="text" size=40
      maxlength=80><br>
      First name:
      <input name="FirstName" type="text" size=40
      maxlength=80><br>
      Address:
      <textarea name="Address" rows=3 cols=40>
      </textarea><br>
      Country:
      <select name="Country" size=1>
        <option>USA
        <option>UK
        <option>Germany
        <option>Other
      </select><br>
      Phone:
      <input name="Tel" type="text" size=40
      maxlength=80><br>
      Fax:
      <input name="Fax" type="text" size=40
      maxlength=80><br>
      E-mail:
      <input name="E-mail" type="text" size=40
      maxlength=80><p>
      <input type="submit" value="Send form">
      <input type="reset" value="Delete form">
    </form>
  </body>
</html>
```

This form is still rather untidy as the individual elements are merged with the continuous text.

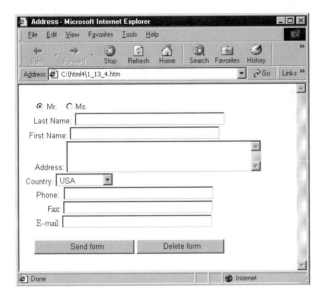

Figure 1.35 *A form should look a bit neater than shown here*

It's always advisable to combine the use of forms and tables. If we correct the formatting of the form using the table functions then the source text might look as follows:

```html
<html>
  <head>
    <title>Address</title>
  </head>
  <body>
    <form method="post" action="mailto:my@address.com">
      <table cols=2>
        <tr>
          <td></td>
          <td>
            <input type="radio" name="title" value="Mr."
            checked>Mr.
            <input type="radio" name="title"
            value="Ms">Ms
          </td>
        </tr>
        <tr>
```

```
      <td>Last name:</td>
      <td><input name="LastName" type="text" size=40
          maxlength=80></td>
   </tr>
   <tr>
      <td>First name:</td>
      <td><input name="FirstName" type="text" size=40
          maxlength=80></td>
   </tr>
   <tr>
      <td>Address:</td>
      <td>
       <textarea name="Address" rows=3 cols=30>
       </textarea>
      </td>
   </tr>
   <tr>
      <td>Country</td>
      <td>
        <select name="Country" size=1>
          <option>USA
          <option>UK
          <option>Germany
          <option>Other
        </select>
      </td>
   </tr>
   <tr>
      <td>Phone:</td>
      <td><input name="Phone" type="text" size=40
          maxlength=80></td>
   </tr>
   <tr>
      <td>Fax:</td>
      <td><input name="Fax" type="text" size=40
          maxlength=80></td>
   </tr>
   <tr>
      <td>E-mail:</td>
      <td><input name="E-mail" type="text" size=40
          maxlength=80></td>
   </tr>
```

```
        <tr>
          <td colspan=2 align="center">
            <input type="submit"
            value="Send form">
            <input type="reset" value="Delete form">
          </td>
        </tr>
      </table>
    </form>
  </body>
</html>
```

If you look at the output of this source text, the form immediately appears much neater and attractive.

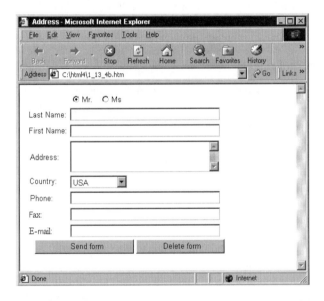

Figure 1.36 *This form is much neater than its predecessor*

1.13.5   Interpreting forms

I've mailed the form we've just seen to demonstrate what the input data looks like. It's all packed into a single line because we might also access a script in the same way and for that all the data must be in one line.

```
title=Mr.&lastname=Bloggs&first-
name=Joe&address=123+Any+Street%0D%0AAny+Town+12345+Cali-
fornia&Country=USA&tel=01234-56789&fax=01234-56790&e-
mail=joe.bloggs@bloggs.com
```

At first sight this looks a bit confusing. But you can see that the form elements are separated by an &. Each form element is assigned a value by means of an = sign. For instance Bloggs has been entered for lastname. When several entries for an element are possible these are each assigned to the element separately. The address field is also very informative. Here you can see that spaces are replaced by a + sign and a line break by the sequence %0D%0A.

Some service providers offer a facility for directly interpreting such forms and forwarding them to your mail address in the correct sequence. Check with your service provider's customer support whether they have such a facility and if so how it works.

1.14 Special tags

You've now had a look at all the important areas HTML offers. There are, however, still a few tags that we haven't mentioned.

1.14.1   Drawing horizontal rules

You can considerably improve the appearance of a page by separating individual sections with horizontal rules. We create these lines using <hr/>. You've already come across this tag in the section "The basics of HTML".

1.14.2   Comments

The source text of an HTML page soon becomes cluttered. It's then often necessary to include comments. Though these appear in the source code they cannot be seen on the page. That's why all browsers ignore text enclosed inside the <!-- ... --> tags.

```
<!-- Outputs the word TEST here. -->
TEST
<!-- This comment remains invisible. -->
```

When you want to make part of your homepage temporarily invisible you can enclose the tags concerned within the comment tags. Removing these tags later on causes the relevant section to reappear.

1.15 Planning before project launch

You now know the basics of HTML programming and can create and publish Internet pages yourself. But before diving straight into programming a homepage you should give some serious thought to content and layout. Now you must be wondering why this section is at the end of the introduction. The answer is quite simple. I'm going to give you some examples that presuppose you're already familiar with HTML.

1.15.1 Considerations before programming

First of all give some thought to the content of your pages. Go through the following checklist and check whether you've thought of everything.

What do I want to convey with my homepage? What should the content be? For example:
- → Private homepage: your hobbies, interests, friends, favorite games, career, in fact anything that you enjoy doing.
- → Club homepage: presentation of the club, the members, events and dates, rules etc.
- → Business homepage: company description, product range, product information, management, employees, delivery times, address, location etc.

Who is the page for?
- → Private homepage: friends, acquaintances, maybe the new employer who saw your homepage address on your job application.
- → Club homepage: members who want the latest news, prospective members who still haven't decided which club to join.
- → Business homepage: the homepage should primarily target customers. It's also of interest to job seekers on the Internet to give them an initial impression of the company.

What must your site achieve?
- → Private homepage: if your homepage does not serve a specific purpose (i.e. a job application) then let your imagination run wild as it's not so important what effect the page has on the visitor. Clearly the main thing is to have fun.
- → Club homepage: the homepage should represent the club and attract new members by making them want to find out more.
- → Business homepage: in this instance the impression the site makes on the visitor is especially important since a customer should feel that the site is geared directly towards them and they should be able to find what they are looking for immediately. Therefore it's very important that the homepage is clearly set out. It's obviously in the company's interest to keep

their product fresh in the customer's mind, especially when they are considering their next purchase. Therefore the effect of advertising has the utmost priority here.

What HTML elements should I use?

→ Private homepage: again the thing is to do what you enjoy.

→ Club homepage: it always makes a good impression if you incorporate some of the club colors into the homepage. And it's also a good idea to enhance the site with graphics.

→ Business homepage: these pages are expected to be right up to date in terms of technology and content. It's therefore advisable to keep abreast of the latest trends which are technically compatible with the appearance of the site. Graphics, tables and forms are part of the basic kit for business homepages.

How compatible must homepages be?

→ Private homepage: if you're using a particular browser and have optimized the site for it just pass this information on to the visitor. The site does not have to be compatible with all browsers.

→ Club homepage: you should optimize the homepage for the most popular browsers (Microsoft Internet Explorer and Netscape Navigator). It's certainly no bad thing to create pages for pure text browsers (though nowadays this is almost redundant).

→ Business homepage: you should aim to get it right for as many visitors as possible. Ensure your pages look the same or at least similar for most of the browsers you know about (and in their different versions). This is the only way you can guarantee a recognition effect. You should bear in mind that many browsers don't support tables, frames or even graphics. Offer these users a suitable compromise. If your site is accessible to overseas customers you ought to be able to present your homepage in their native language.

What are the limitations of Internet sites?

→ Generally speaking, and this applies to all homepages, an Internet site can never replace a face-to-face meeting. Its purpose is to inform and encourage personal contact.

→ There are some legal restrictions. Observe the laws of the country you publish your pages in. For example, not everything you can write in the USA will be permitted in the United Kingdom. You should always bear in mind that your homepage will be viewed across the world and you should conduct yourself in such a way that does not throw you and the institutions you represent into a bad light.

1.15.2 Programming

Once you know what content you want to publish you can concentrate on the programming.

File structure

To start with you should think of a file structure that will make your work easier. It usually makes sense to divide large projects into subgroups. I'd like to illustrate this procedure with a couple of examples.

If you want to create a private homepage it's very useful to separate the graphics files from the HTML files so as not to lose the overall view. A simple file structure would then appear thus:

Figure 1.37 *A simple file structure typical for small homepages*

If you create the file index.htm in the homepage directory you can add graphics in this form:

```
<html>
  <head>
    <title>A small homepage</title>
  </head>
  <body>
    This graphic is in its own directory:<br/>
    <img src="graphic/an_image.gif"><br/>
  </body>
</html>
```

As this file is in the homepage directory, then like the graphics directory it's sufficient for the directory name to begin with graphics/... since if it begins with homepage/graphics/... the browser will look for a homepage directory in the directory of the same name.

Even if you're programming under Windows and are used to using the backslash (\) as the separator for directory names you should use the normal slash (/) here as this is used in UNIX systems. Since most servers are based on this system it's advisable to pay attention to this detail. A current browser will therefore run smoothly under Windows and when it comes across a slash it will interpret this as a backslash when necessary.

I'd like to mention a further example for readers who want to create a business homepage. These pages are normally very complex and therefore require a well thought out file structure.

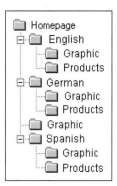

Figure 1.38 *A business homepage often consists of a lot of data and you should save it in a well organized manner*

In this case we have a homepage in three languages containing graphic elements and a large number of product descriptions. As you see we have created a subdirectory for each language which in turn contains the `graphic` and `products` subdirectories. In addition there is a folder called `graphic` in the root directory of the homepage.

Of course you're now wondering how to handle this kind of file structure and why there's a graphics directory outside the language folders if they already have one themselves. If you imagine the homepage of a hardware manufacturer whose site is available in these three languages some of the graphics will be the same in each language. These include the company logo and photos of the hardware and workers and so on. However some will be graphical menus. The company will use these as anchors for links and they will often contain text. These labels will obviously be different in the individual languages.

The start page `index.htm` in the root directory `homepage` will look something like this:

```
<html>
  <head>
    <title>Bloggs Hardware Inc.</title>
  </head>
  <body>
    <center>
      <img src="graphics/logo.gif"
      alt="Bloggs Hardware Inc.">
```

```
        </center>
        <p/>
        Welcome to our homepage. Please choose a
        language:<br/>
        <a href="german/index.htm">German</a><br/>
        <a href="english/index.htm">English</a><br/>
        <a href="spanish/index.htm">Spanish</a><br/>
    </body>
</html>
```

The company logo which is in the general graphics folder appears on the screen. The visitor is then asked what language he wants to view the site in. Once he clicks on a language the browser displays the welcome page in the chosen language. It's advisable to give the different language versions of a particular page the same name. Here the welcome page is called index.htm in each language. The major advantage of this is that we can copy the HTML structure of a page for the other languages and so we only have to translate the text. Here is an example:

The welcome page in English looks like this:

```
<html>
    <head>
        <title>Bloggs Hardware Inc. (English)</title>
    </head>
    <body>
        <center>
            <img src="../graphics/logo.gif"
            alt="Bloggs Hardware Inc.">
        </center>
        <p/>
        Welcome to the English homepage of
        Bloggs Hardware Inc.<p/>


        We offer a wide range of hardware. Please visit our
        <a href="products/list.htm">product list </a> for more
information <br/>
        Please click
        <a href="../index.htm">here</a> to
        choose another language.<br/>
        Please feel free to send an
        <a href="mailto:info@bloggshardware.com">
        <img src="graphics/mail.gif" alt="e-mail"></a>.
```

```
    </body>
</html>
```

We can now copy this file into the German folder and simply translate the displayed text which looks like this:

```
<html>
  <head>
    <title>Bloggs Hardware Inc. (German)</title>
  </head>
  <body>
    <center>
      <img src="../graphics/logo.gif"
      alt="Bloggs Hardware Inc.">
    </center>
    <p/>
    Wilkommen auf der deutschsprachigen homepage der
    Bloggs Hardware Inc.<p/>
    Wir bieten Ihnen ein umfangreiches Angebot an Hardware.
Bitte verschaffen Sie sich einen Überblick in unserer
    <a href="products/list.htm">Produktliste</a>.
    <br/>
    Hier gelangen Sie wieder <a href="../index.htm">zurück</
a> zur
    Sprachanwahl.<br/>
    Sie können uns gerne eine
    <a href="mailto:info@bloggshardware.com">
    <img src="graphics/mail.gif" alt="E-Mail"></a>
schreiben.
  </body>
</html>
```

Only the text which appears on the screen has changed. The basic structure and the link addresses remain exactly the same. This has the enormous advantage that you only have to think a page through once and then translate it one by one into another language.

Let's look at a few of the details. At the start the company logo appears again. We add it using the HTML line `<img src="../graphics/logo.gif" alt="Bloggs Hardware Inc.">`. This line stays the same for all languages since it makes no difference which of the three language folders contain these lines. The two dots at the start of the image address mean we can find the `graphics` folder in the parent folder (in this case `homepage`). You'll certainly know the command `cd ..` from older operating systems. `cd` means 'change directory' and the two dots mean 'go up' one level, to the folder that contains the one you're in now. Therefore simply save the company logo in the folder `homepage/graphics`. This saves storage space on the server. We then draw attention to the company's product list by using `<a href="products/list.htm">product list</a>`. This resides in the relevant `products` subdirectory of the individual language folders. As the filename of the list in each of these directories is the same it's sufficient to translate the words "product list" and leave the rest the same:

```
<a href="products/list.htm">Produktliste</a>
```

At the end of the page we give the site visitor the option of writing an e-mail to Bloggs Hardware:

```
<a href="mailto:info@bloggshardware.com">
<img src="graphics/mail.gif" alt="e-mail"></a>
```

A graphic acts as an anchor. It resides in the relevant graphics file of the individual language folders. These are graphics containing text and so are different for each language. In this example "e-mail" in English is written in lower case and in German in upper case ("E-Mail"). The address `graphics/mail.gif` however remains the same on all three pages since the file `mail.gif` is always found in the correct graphics folder. Note that in the case of images you can always give a text as an alternative for pure text browsers (`alt="e-mail"`). You must always include this in the translation otherwise a visitor with a text browser will be left somewhat in the dark.

Once you've thought out a suitable file structure you'll always have an overview of your files and this can save a lot of time if you need to reuse HTML texts.

Clear programming

Clarity in HTML texts is essential for making quick corrections. Therefore I'd like to give you a few tips on how best to implement fairly large pages in HTML so you can find your way about in them again afterwards without any problems.

First of all you should get used to indenting text between an opening and closing tag. A typical HTML file might then look like:

```
<html>
  <head>
    <title>A homepage</title>
  </head>
  <body>
    <center>
      <img src="an_image.gif">
      <br/>
      This text is centered and
```

```
        <b>this passage is in bold type.</b>
        <br/>
      </center>
      A <a href="page2.htm">link</a>
      you can write in a single line without
      hesitation.
    </body>
</html>
```

Laying out your source text in this way you'll soon realize whether you've forgotten a closing tag and will be able to see at first glance, for instance, how much of the text is centered. However, you should only indent larger sections since you can write smaller passages (such as links or the page title) in a single line without any problem.

There is another way of getting structure into HTML texts that you've already come across in the section "Special tags" and that is to use comments. In fairly long texts with a little imagination you can produce paragraphs that really stand out:

```
<html>
  <!-- ************************* -->
  <!-- * Here is the start of the head * -->
  <!-- ************************* -->
  <head>
    ...
  </head>
  <!-- ************************** -->
  <!-- * Here is the start of the body * -->
  <!-- ************************** -->
  <body>
    ...
  </body>
</html>
```

Bear in mind these methods and you'll be able to find you're way about in your source text even years later. Sometimes it's even necessary to apply this way of programming if you're not the only person amending the pages. You should then agree with your fellow programmers what programming method you want to stick to so you don't have to wade unnecessarily through someone else's HTML texts when these have been done one way by one programmer and another way by another.

1.15.3 Visual appearance

If you look around on the Internet you'll realize that homepages have taken on a certain appearance. There are various aspects you should take note of in this respect when designing a user-friendly homepage.

Text

If you want to make your site look good it's important that the text is well formatted and appears in a readable form. I've listed a few tips on this below:

→ Make sure the contrast between text and background is as strong as possible. Use black text on light backgrounds and white text on dark as often as you can.

→ Even though you might have a large number of different fonts you should limit yourself to one or two per page otherwise these become very confusing.

→ Headings add structure to long texts. For the longer sections you can increase the effect with horizontal rules.

Links

The most important elements of a homepage are the links to other pages. Therefore there's also often a separate area for bringing together all the important links to other pages. There are a number of ways of doing this:

→ You can display the links on the left-hand side one underneath another. Use either frames or a table with just the links in the left-hand column and the actual page in the right-hand column. This gives the visitor an index to move through.

1

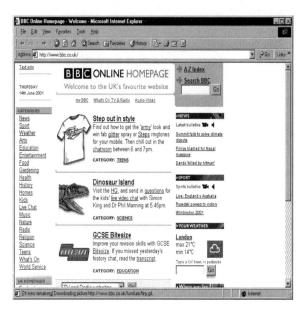

Figure 1.39 *The BBC online homepage displays links on the left-hand side*

As many browsers don't display frames or tables you can also place the links at the end of the page in continuous text. It looks like this:

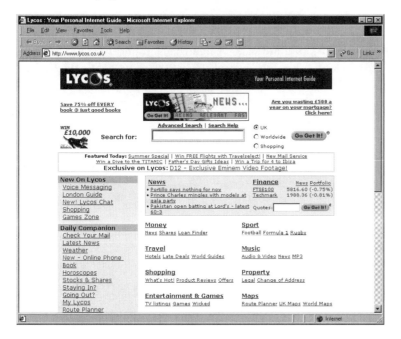

Figure 1.40 *Even old browsers will display this list of links correctly making it easier for the visitor*

As you can see from the Lycos homepage, there's another point you should bear in mind. It makes a good impression if you add navigation buttons at the top or bottom of your homepage. The visitor can then move easily onto the next page and will always find the way back. These buttons are usually located at the top or bottom of a homepage.

Graphics

If you're using graphics in your pages you should note a number of aspects to make these really effective.

Graphics should never be too large. This increases the loading time of the page. If necessary reduce the resolution, the number of colors or the size of the graphics. Sometimes it helps to use another format. Save your graphics in various formats and compare the size of the files.

Match the graphics you use to the style of the page. An image in loud colors can quite quickly mar an otherwise very conservative page.

When you add graphics you should take care that they blend in with the background. Sometimes it makes a lot of sense to set the graphics to a transparent background.

Background images shouldn't be too colorful. If you choose a dark background then keep the other colors quite dark. A light background works best when there are no dark colors. Failure to observe this will soon make the page unreadable since the text continues to work on the other background and that makes reading difficult.

Part I

Take That!

Quick reference section

This quick reference section should clarify which attributes belong to the individual tags and their effect. A fundamental feature of HTML programming is the compatibility of the individual tags with diverse browsers. I have made a list of the location of all tags and their attributes in Microsoft Internet Explorer and Netscape Navigator as well as in applicable HTML versions. The version name "4.0B1" refers to the browser version 4.0 Beta 1. This reference covers information up to the browser version Microsoft Internet Explorer 5.02 (version 5.5 appeared too late to be covered in this book) and Netscape Navigator 4.72.

2.1 Subject summary

Below is a summary of all tags sorted according to subject areas.

HTML structure
```
<body>, <head>, <html>, <frameset>
```

Head elements
```
<base>, <isindex>, <link>, <meta>, <nextid>, <scripts>,
<style>, <title>
```

Hyperlinks
```
<a>
```

Line breaks
```
<br>, <nobr>, <wbr>
```

Formatting paragraphs
```
<address>, <blockquote>, <center>, <cite>, <code>, <dfn>,
<h1>, <h2>, <h3>, <h4>, <h5>, <h6>, <marquee>, <multicol>,
<p>, <pre>
```

Formatting typeface

`<abbr>`, `<b>`, `<big>`, `<blink>`, `<em>`, `<font>`, `<i>`, `<kbd>`, `<q>`, `<s>`, `<samp>`, `<small>`, `<strike>`, `<strong>`, `<sub>`, `<sup>`, `<tt>`, `<u>`, `<var>`

Listen

`<dd>`, `<dir>`, `<dl>`, `<dt>`, `<li>`, `<menu>`, `<ol>`, `<ul>`

Tables

`<caption>`, `<col>`, `<colgroup>`, `<thead>`, `<tbody>`, `<tfoot>`, `<table>`, `<th>`, `<td>`, `<tr>`

Forms

`<button>`, `<fieldset>`, `<form>`, `<input>`, `<keygen>`, `<label>`, `<legend>`, `<optgroup>`, `<option>`, `<select>`, `<text area>`

Frames

`<frame>`, `<frameset>`, `<noframes>`

Multimedia elements

`<area>`, `<bgsound>`, `<img>`, `<map>`, `<object>`

Embedded objects

`<applet>`, `<embed>`, `<iframe>`, `<noembed>`, `<noscript>`, `<param>`, `<script>`

Revision

`<del>`, `<ins>`

2.2   A

2.2.1   *<a>*

Tag/Attribute	2.0	3.0	3.2	4.0	Internet Explorer	Netscape
`<a href>`	X	X	X	X	1.0	1.0
accesskey				X	4.0B1	
charset				X		
coords				X		
hreflang				X		
methods	X	X				
name	X	X	X	X	1.0	1.0

Tag/Attribute	2.0	3.0	3.2	4.0	Internet Explorer	Netscape
rel	X	X	X	X		
rev	X	X	X	X		
shape		X		X		
tabindex				X	4.0BI	
target				X	3.0AI	2.0
title	X	X	X	X	4.0BI	
type				X		
urn	X	X				

The most important tag in HTML is <a>, as it defines a link (in conjunction with the attribute href) to other HTML pages or other data. A text area or another object is given as an anchor for the link.

accesskey

You can define a shortcut key to access the link using accesskey. Assign the attribute a single letter and it will be executed when you hit this key with the appropriate shortcut key. This key is dependent on the browser and operational system.

charset

This attribute contains the character coding of the target. The standard value is ISO-8859-1.

coords

Gives the coordinates for the anchor area of the link in an image map. Depending on the value of the attribute shape the coordinates are given as follows (always in pixels starting from the left upper corner of the image):

Value of shape	Opening format coords
rectangle	"left, upper, right, lower"
circle	"center X, center Y, Radius"
polygon	"point1 X, point1 Y, point2 X, point2 Y, etc."

Table 2.1 *Opening format coords depend on value of shape*

href

The target address of the link.

> **Warning** Either href or name must be defined in <a>.

hreflang

This attribute states the main target language.

methods

This should originally have been a list of target key words separated by spaces. However, because no current browser can support this attribute it was no longer included after HTML 3.2.

name

A description of the link (with an additional bookmark function), which enables the user to jump to this position in the document is given here.

> **Warning** Either href or name must be defined in <a>.

rel

This should originally have been a list of target key words separated by spaces, which clarify the link between the page and the target. Unfortunately no current browser can support this attribute.

rev

This attribute corresponds to the reversal of rel. This should originally have been a list of target key words separated by spaces, which clarify the link between the target and the page. Unfortunately no current browser can support this attribute.

shape

The geometric form of the anchor area in image maps is set here. Possible values are default (standard value), rectangle (rectangle), circle (circle) and polygon (polygon).

tabindex

Gives the tab index of the link. Positive values correspond to the position of the link in the list of objects which can be activated by ⇥ . Negative values mean that the link does not appear in the tab index.

target

The name of the target frame, in which the target link should be displayed is listed here. *Magic Target Names = SAMS Pg 415*

title

_blank = new window & _top = fill whole window

Gives the target title, which is displayed when the user moves the mouse over the link without clicking.

type

Gives the MIME target type.

urn

This attribute was originally supposed to supplement name, but was never supported by the current browsers and therefore disappeared from the language as of HTML 3.2.

Example:

```
<a href="http://www.address.com/index/index.htm#PointA"
target="Center frame">Click here!</a>
```

Tag/Attribute	2.0	3.0	3.2	4.0	Internet Explorer	Netscape
`<a name>`	X	X	X	X	1.0	1.0
`href`	X	X	X	X	1.0	1.0
`methods`	X	X				
`name`	X	X	X	X	1.0	1.0
`rel`	X	X	X	X		
`rev`	X	X	X	X		
`title`	X	X	X	X	4.0B1	
`urn`	X	X				

One of the most important tags in HTML is `<a>`, as it defines (with the attribute name) a bookmark.

href

The target address of the link.

Warning Either `href` or `name` must be defined in `<a>`.

methods

This should originally have been a list of target key words separated by spaces. However because no current browser can support this attribute it was no longer included after HTML 3.2.

name

A description for the bookmark, which enables the user to jump directly to this position in the document is given here.

Warning Either `href` or `name` must be defined in `<a>`.

rel

This should originally have been a list of target key words separated by spaces, which clarify the link between the page and the target. Unfortunately no current browser can support this attribute.

rev

This attribute corresponds to the reversal of `rel`. This should originally have been a list of target key words separated by spaces, which clarify the link between the target and the page. Unfortunately no current browser can support this attribute.

title

Gives the title of the target which is displayed when the user moves the mouse over the link without clicking.

urn

This attribute was originally supposed to supplement `name`, but was never supported by the current browsers and therefore disappeared from the language as of HTML 3.2.

Example:

```
<a name="PointA">
```

2.2.2   *<abbr>*

Tag/Attribute	2.0	3.0	3.2	4.0	Internet Explorer	Netscape
`<abbr>`				X		
`title`				X		

This tag marks abbreviations. This function can be useful when using, e.g. search engines.

title

Gives the full description of the abbreviation.

Example:

```
<abbr title="Zip code">ZIP</abbr>
```

See:

`<b>`, `<big>`, `<blink>`, `<em>`, `<font>`, `<i>`, `<kbd>`, `<q>`, `<s>`, `<samp>`, `<small>`, `<strike>`, `<strong>`, `<sub>`, `<sup>`, `<tt>`, `<u>`, `<var>`

2.2.3   *<acronym>*

Tag/Attribute	2.0	3.0	3.2	4.0	Internet Explorer	Netscape
`<acronym>`				X	4.0	
`title`				X	4.0	

This tag marks abbreviations. This function can be useful when using, e.g. search engines.

title

Gives the full description of the abbreviation.

Example:

```
<acronym title="Zip Code">ZIP</acronym>
```

2.2.4   *<address>*

Tag/Attribute	2.0	3.0	3.2	4.0	Internet Explorer	Netscape
`<address>`	X	X	X	X	1.0	1.0

This tag is specifically for framing addresses. This is generally presented in italics and indented.

Example:

```
<address>
  Max Jones<br>
  Jones Street 123<br>
  12345 Jonestown<br>
</address>
```

See:

`<blockquote>`, `<center>`, `<cite>`, `<code>`, `<dfn>`, `<h1>`, `<h2>`, `<h3>`, `<h4>`, `<h5>`, `<h6>`, `<marquee>`, `<multicol>`, `<p>`, `<pre>`

2.2.5   *<applet>*

Tag/Attribute	2.0	3.0	3.2	4.0	Internet Explorer	Netscape
`<applet>`			X	X	3.0B2	2.0
`align`			X	X	3.0B2	2.0
`alt`			X	X	3.0B2	2.0
`archive`				X	4.0	3.0B7
`code`			X	X	3.0B2	2.0
`codebase`			X	X	3.0B2	2.0
`height`			X	X	3.0B2	2.0
`hspace`			X	X	3.0B2	2.0
`mayscript`						3.0
`name`			X	X	3.0B2	2.0
`object`				X		
`src`					4.0	
`vspace`			X	X	3.0B2	2.0
`width`			X	X	3.0B2	2.0

This tag is used to include Java applets. Browsers which support Java ignore all instructions included in `<applet>` ... `</applet>` except for `<param>`tags. Browsers which do not support Java ignore `<applet>` and `<param>`, which are found within these tags. They show all other instructions contained in `<applet>` ... `</applet>`. This is also the case if the Java applet creates an error and cannot be loaded.

align

Gives the alignment of the following text to applet. Possible values: `baseline`, `bottom`, `left`, `middle`, `right`, `textbottom`, `textmiddle`, `texttop` and `top`.

alt

The value of this text is given when the browser does not recognize `<applet>`. This is for example true for old text browsers.

archive

Refers to a `.zip` file, containing all applet classes. The URL is given relative to `codebase` or completely.

code

Refers to the applet class. The URL is given relative to `codebase` or completely.

codebase

Gives the index, in which the code can be found and to which the `archive`, `code` and `src` should refer.

height

Gives the height of the applet in pixels. This means that when the code is being downloaded a free variable parameter of the appropriate size is displayed.

hspace

Gives the left and right applet gap to all other HTML components in pixels.

mayscript

This attribute has no value. When it is given, the applet Java Script functionality is activated. If the attribute is missing and the applet attempts to gain access to Java Script elements, an error occurs.

name

This attribute contains the applet name. This is used as proof of identification for other applets on this page.

object

Gives the name of a data source, containing applet.

src

Refers to the applet class. The URL is given relative to `codebase` or completely.

vspace

Gives the upper and lower applet gaps to all other HTML components in pixels.

width

Gives the width of the applet in pixels. This means that when the code is being downloaded a free variable parameter of the appropriate size is displayed.

Example:

```
<applet codebase="http://www.address.com/java/"
code="an_applet.class" >
  <param name="Line1" value="Text line 1">
  <param name="Line2" value="Text line 2">
  <param name="Line2" value="Text line 2">
  Your browser is not Java compatible!<br>
</applet>
```

See:

`<param>`, `<embed>`, `<iframe>`, `<noembed>`, `<noscript>`, `<param>`, `<script>`

2.2.6   *<area>*

Tag/Attribute	2.0	3.0	3.2	4.0	Internet Explorer	Netscape
`<area>`			X	X	1.0	2.0
`accesskey`				X		
`alt`			X	X	4.0B2	3.0
`coords`			X	X	1.0	2.0
`href`			X	X	1.0	2.0
`nohref`			X	X	1.0	2.0
`shape`			X	X	1.0	2.0
`tabindex`				X	4.0B1	
`target`				X	3.0A1	2.0

This tag is necessary for the production of image maps for the client. Hot areas can be produced in these maps.

accesskey

You can define a shortcut key to access the link using `accesskey`. Assign the attribute a single letter and it will be executed when you hit this key with the appropriate shortcut key. This key is dependent on the browser and operational system.

alt

The value of this attribute is given, if the browser does not recognize `<area>`. This is true for the old text browsers.

coords

Gives the coordinates for the link anchor area in an image map. Depending on the value of the attribute `shape`, the coordinates are given as follows (always in pixels starting from the left upper corner of the image):

Value of shape	Opening format for coords
rectangle	"left, upper, right, lower"
circle	"center X, center Y, radius"
polygon	"point1 X, point1 Y, point2 X, point2 Y, etc."

Table 2.2 *Opening format for coords depends on value of shape*

href

Gives the target of the link.

> **Warning** May not be placed together with `nohref`!

nohref

If you would like to turn off an `<area>` link temporarily, you can use this sole attribute instead of `href`.

shape

The geometric form of the anchor area in the image maps is set here. Possible values are `default` (Standard value), `rectangle` (rectangle), `circle` (circle) and `polygon` (polygon).

tabindex

Gives the tab index for the hot area. Positive values correspond to the position of the link in the list of objects which can be activated by ⇥ . Negative values mean that the link does not appear in the tab index.

target

The name of the target frame, in which the target of the link should be displayed, is listed here.

Example:

```
<map name="An image map">
  <area shape="rectangle" coords="10,20,30,40"
  href="http://www.address.com/a.htm">
  <area shape="circle" COORDS="60,50,20" href="
```

```
   http://www.address.com/b.htm ">
   <area shape="polygon" coords="5,100,10,110,0,110" href="
   http://www.address.com/c.htm ">
</map>
```

See:

```
<bgsound>, <img>, <map>, <object>
```

2.3   B

2.3.1   <b>

Tag/Attribute	2.0	3.0	3.2	4.0	Internet Explorer	Netscape
<b>	X	X	X	X	1.0	1.0

Text, which appears within <b> ... </b>, shall be in bold.

Example:

```
<b>This text shall be printed in bold,</b> but this will
not.
```

See:

```
<abbr>, <big>, <blink>, <em>, <font>, <i>, <kbd>, <q>, <s>,
<samp>, <small>, <strike>, <strong>, <sub>, <sup>, <tt>,
<u>, <var>
```

2.3.2   <base>

Tag/Attribute	2.0	3.0	3.2	4.0	Internet Explorer	Netscape
<base>	X	X	X	X	1.0	1.0
href	X	X	X	X	1.0	1.0
target				X	3.0A1	2.0

This tag enables the user to access the basic settings of href and target for all HTML elements of the page.

href

Gives the base address, containing all relative URL instructions for the page.

target

Gives the standard target frame, automatically referring to all HTML elements in the page.

Example:

```
<base href="http://www.address.com" target="Center frame">
```

See:

```
<isindex>, <link>, <meta>, <nextid>, <scripts>, <style>,
<title>
```

2.3.3   *<basefont>*

Tag/Attribute	2.0	3.0	3.2	4.0	Internet Explorer	Netscape
`<basefont>`			X	X	1.0	1.0
`color`				X	1.0	
`face`				X	1.0	
`size`			X	X	1.0	1.0

This tag sets the standard typeface.

color

The color of the text is set here. RGB values and, for many browsers, predefined color values (see Appendix B) are the standard.

face

A list of the names of typeface separated by commas. When the appropriate typeface has been found (and installed in the system) it will be used as standard typeface for the text contained in this tag.

size

Represents the size of type. Valid values : 1 to 7. If the user gives precedence to the value + or to a -, the size will be calculated relative to the actual size of the typeface.

Example:

```
<basefont color="#ff0000" face="Arial" size=4>
```

2.3.4   *<bdo>*

Tag/Attribute	2.0	3.0	3.2	4.0	Internet Explorer	Netscape
`<bdo>`				X	5.0B2	
`dir`				X	5.0B2	
`lang`				X	5.0B2	

This tag stands for "bi-directional override". It is used when languages, written from left to right or languages, read from right to left appear in the same HTML document.

dir

Gives the direction in which the text block is written. The following values are possible:

Value	Meaning
ltr	From left to right.
rtl	From right to left.

Table 2.3 *The values of dir in <bdo>*

lang

Gives the language of the text block.

Example:

```
This is forwards and <bdo dir="rtl">this is backwards</
bdo>.
```

2.3.5   *<bgsound>*

Tag/Attribute	2.0	3.0	3.2	4.0	Internet Explorer	Netscape
<bgsound>					2.0	
balance					4.0BI	
delay					2.0	
loop					2.0	
src					2.0	
volume					2.0BI	

This tag enables the user to play background music.

balance

This attribute allows the user to influence the alignment of the music reproduction via the stereo. Values between -10000 (left) and 10000 (right) are allowed. A balanced stereo sound reproduction can be obtained using the value 0.

delay

Gives the delay before play and between repeats in milliseconds.

loop

Gives the number of repeats. Valid values are positive whole numbers or `infinite` for a continuous repeat.

src

The URL expects an audio file (`.au`, `.mid` or `.wav`).

volume

Gives the volume of the sound reproduction. Possible values: `-10000` (quiet or off) to `0` (full volume).

Example:

```
<bgsound src="a_song.mid" loop=infinite>
```

See:

```
<area>, <img>, <map>, <object>
```

2.3.6 *<big>*

Tag/Attribute	2.0	3.0	3.2	4.0	Internet Explorer	Netscape
`<big>`		X	X	X	3.0A1	1.1

Text which appears within `<big> ... </big>` shall be in larger type.

Example:

```
<big>This text will be in larger letters,</big> but this
will not.
```

See:

```
<abbr>, <b>, <blink>, <em>, <font>, <i>, <kbd>, <q>, <s>,
<samp>, <small>, <strike>, <strong>, <sub>, <sup>, <tt>,
<u>, <var>
```

2.3.7 *<blink>*

Tag/Attribute	2.0	3.0	3.2	4.0	Internet Explorer	Netscape
`<blink>`					4.0B1	1.0

This tag activates a flashing function in the framed text block.

Example:

```
<blink>ALARM!</blink>
```

See:

```
<abbr>, <b>, <big>, <em>, <font>, <i>, <kbd>, <q>, <s>,
```

`<samp>`, `<small>`, `<strike>`, `<strong>`, `<sub>`, `<sup>`, `<tt>`, `<u>`, `<var>`

2.3.8   *<blockquote>*

Tag/Attribute	2.0	3.0	3.2	4.0	Internet Explorer	Netscape
`<blockquote>`	X	X	X	X	1.0	1.0
cite				X		

Marks quotes. These are generally indented on the left and right side.

cite

Gives the original quote address as URL.

Example:

```
<blockquote cite="http://www.spectrosoftware.com">...and
life becomes colorful </blockquote>.
```

See:

`<address>`, `<center>`, `<cite>`, `<code>`, `<dfn>`, `<h1>`, `<h2>`, `<h3>`, `<h4>`, `<h5>`, `<h6>`, `<marquee>`, `<multicol>`, `<p>`, `<pre>`.

2.3.9   *<body>*

Tag/Attribute	2.0	3.0	3.2	4.0	Internet Explorer	Netscape
`<body>`	X	X	X	X	1.0	1.0
alink			X	X	4.0B1	1.1
background		X	X	X	1.0	1.1
bgcolor			X	X	1.0	1.1
bgproperties					2.0	
bottommargin					4.0B1	
leftmargin					2.0	
link			X	X	1.0	1.1
marginheight						4.0
marginwidth						4.0
no wrap					4.0	
rightmargin					4.0B1	
scroll					4.0B1	
text			X	X	1.0	1.1
topmargin					2.0	

Tag/Attribute	2.0	3.0	3.2	4.0	Internet Explorer	Netscape
vlink			X	X	1.0	1.1

This tag is used to structure the HTML page to its highest level. All text and image elements should be enclosed by `<body>` ... `</body>`, as global attributes, which have an effect on the entire HTML body are defined in this index.

alink

The color of a current link (link on the page) is set here. RGB values and, for many browsers, predefined color values (see Appendix B) are the standard.

background

Gives the address of the image, which should be loaded onto the background of the HTML page.

bgcolor

The background color of the document is set here. RGB values and, for many browsers, predefined color values (see Appendix B) are the standard.

bgproperties

Gives background features. The only valid value, which does not affect the background even when scrolling is currently `fixed`. The content of the page moves in the same way as a transparent over the background.

bottommargin

Gives the bottom margin of the document in pixels.

leftmargin

Gives the left margin of the document in pixels.

link

The color of a link is set here. RGB values and, for many browsers, predefined color values (see Appendix B) are the standard.

marginheight

Gives the upper and lower margin of the document in pixels.

marginwidth

Gives the left and right margin of the document in pixels.

no wrap

Gives information as to whether the normal HTML word wrap rules are valid or should be ignored.

Value	Meaning
false	The normal rules apply: text, which has come to the end of the line, will be automatically wrapped.
true	Text, which has come to the end of the line, will not be wrapped. Exceptions will only be made in the case of specified formatting (` `, `<p>`, etc)

Table 2.4 *The values of no wrap in <body>*

rightmargin

Gives the right margin of the document in pixels.

scroll

Gives information as to whether the scroll bar should be displayed.

Value	Meaning
auto	Scroll bar should appear when necessary.
no	Scroll bar should never appear.
yes	Scroll bar should always appear.

Table 2.5 *The value of scroll in <body>*

text

The color of the text is set here. RGB values and, for many browsers, predefined color values (see Appendix B) are the standard.

topmargin

Gives the upper margin of the document in pixels.

vlink

The color of a link, which has already been accessed, is set here. RGB values and, for many browsers, predefined color values (see Appendix B) are the standard.

Example:

```
<html>
  <head>
    <!-- Information on the content is given here.-->
  </head>
  <body>
    The content is listed here.
  </body>
</html>
```

See:

```
<head>, <html>, <frameset>
```

2.3.10 *
*

Tag/Attribute	2.0	3.0	3.2	4.0	Internet Explorer	Netscape
` `	X	X	X	X	1.0	1.0
`clear`			X	X	1.0	1.0

This tag produces an obligatory word wrap.

clear

This attribute was supplemented to be able to work with images, which are moved left or right by the attribute `align` in `<img>`. It can be used when working with all objects, which are moved by `align`.

Value	Meaning
`none`	A normal word wrap is produced.
`left`	The line is wrapped and the next line should be inserted in such a way that the left border is free of images (or other objects).
`right`	The line is wrapped and the next line should be inserted in such a way that the right border is free of images (or other objects).
`all`	The line is wrapped and the next line should be inserted in such a way that all borders are free of images (or other objects).

Table 2.6 *The value of* `clear` *in* `<br>`

Example:

```
This is the first line<br>
and this the second.
```

See:

```
<nobr>, <wbr>
```

2.3.11   <button>

Tag/Attribute	2.0	3.0	3.2	4.0	Internet Explorer	Netscape
<button>				X	4.0B1	
accesskey				X	4.0B1	
disabled				X	4.0B1	
name				X	4.0B1	
tabindex				X	4.0B1	
type				X	4.0B1	
value				X	4.0B1	

This tag can produce buttons in forms.

accesskey

You can define a shortcut key to access the button using accesskey. Assign the attribute a single letter and it will be executed when you hit this key with the appropriate shortcut key. This key is dependent on the browser and operational system.

disabled

This sole attribute ensures that the button is registered as inactive and prevents the button from functioning.

name

Gives the description of the button, so that it can be identified when script is opened.

tabindex

Gives the tab index of the button. Positive values stand for the position of the button in the list of objects activated by ⇥ . Negative values mean that the button does not appear in the tab index.

type

States which function the button should have in the form.

Value	Meaning
button	Defines the button as multifunctional (the button is assigned its own script.)
reset	The button deletes the form.
submit	The button sends the data on the form.

Table 2.7 *The value of type in <button>*

value

Gives the value of the button, which should be submitted to the script, when it was activated.

Example:

```
<button type="submit" name="dispatch" tabindex=1>
  <img SRC="an image.gif">
</button>
```

See:

`<fieldset>`, `<form>`, `<input>`, `<keygen>`, `<label>`, `<legend>`, `<optgroup>`, `<option>`, `<select>`, `<textarea>`

2.4 C

2.4.1 *<caption>*

Tag/Attribute	2.0	3.0	3.2	4.0	Internet Explorer	Netscape
`<caption>`		X	X	X	2.0	1.1
`align`		X	X	X	2.0	1.1
`valign`					2.0	

This tag can only be used within `<table>` ... `</table>` and has the same status as `<tr>`. It produces a table heading or a signature on the entire table range.

align

Gives the alignment within the table cells.

Value	Meaning
`bottom`	The content is aligned to the bottom. (In the Internet Explorer using valign!)
`top`	The content is aligned to the top. (In the Internet Explorer using valign!)
`center`	The content is aligned in the center. (Only in Internet Explorer!)
`left`	The content is aligned to the left. (Only in Internet Explorer!)
`right`	The content is aligned to the right. (Only in Internet Explorer!)

Table 2.8 *The value of align in <caption>*

valign

Gives the vertical alignment within the table cells.

Value	Meaning
bottom	The content is aligned to the bottom.
top	The content is aligned to the top.

Table 2.9 *The value of valign in <caption>*

Example:

```
<table border=1>
  <caption>Browser statistic</caption>
  <tr><th>Browser</th><th>Market share</th></tr>
  <tr><td>Microsoft Internet Explorer</td><td>60.4 %</td>
  </tr>
  <tr><td>Netscape Communicator</td><td>38.5 %</td></tr>
  <tr><td>others</td><td>1.1 %</td></tr>
</table>
```

See:

```
<col>, <colgroup>, <thead>, <tbody>, <tfoot>, <table>,
<th>, <td>, <tr>
```

2.4.2   <center>

Tag/Attribute	2.0	3.0	3.2	4.0	Internet Explorer	Netscape
<center>			X	X	1.0	1.0

Centers a text block including all other HTML elements.

Example:

```
This text is aligned to the left<br>
<center>and this text is centered.</center>
```

See:

```
<address>, <blockquote>, <cite>, <code>, <dfn>, <h1>, <h2>,
<h3>, <h4>, <h5>, <h6>, <marquee>, <multicol>, <p>, <pre>
```

2.4.3   <cite>

Tag/Attribute	2.0	3.0	3.2	4.0	Internet Explorer	Netscape
<cite>	X	X	X	X	1.0	1.0

Marked quotes. These are generally printed in italics.

Example:

```
<cite>...and life becomes colorful</cite>
```

See:

```
<address>, <blockquote>, <center>, <code>, <dfn>, <h1>,
<h2>, <h3>, <h4>, <h5>, <h6>, <marquee>, <multicol>, <p>,
<pre>
```

2.4.4   <code>

Tag/Attribute	2.0	3.0	3.2	4.0	Internet Explorer	Netscape
<code>	X	X	X	X	1.0	1.0

This tag formats the source code. This is generally shown in a typeface, which produces letters of identical width.

Example:

```
<code>if(x==y) return;</code>
```

See:

```
<address>, <blockquote>, <center>, <cite>, <dfn>, <h1>,
<h2>, <h3>, <h4>, <h5>, <h6>, <marquee>, <multicol>, <p>,
<pre>
```

2.4.5   <col>

Tag/Attribute	2.0	3.0	3.2	4.0	Internet Explorer	Netscape
<col>				X	3.0A1	
align				X	4.0B1	
bgcolor					4.0	
char				X		
charoff				X		
span				X	3.0A1	
valign				X	4.0B1	
width				X	3.0A1	

This tag represents a supplement to the common tables. Basic settings for the columns in the table are set here. This tag always stands inside a <colgroup> ... </colgroup> image. No data is added here, but sometimes formatting.

align

Gives the horizontal alignment within the column.

Value	Meaning
center	The content is aligned in the center.
left	The content is aligned to the left.
right	The content is aligned to the right.

Table 2.10 *The value of align in <col>*

bgcolor

The background color of the column is set here. RGB values and, for many browsers, predefined color values (see Appendix B) are the standard.

char

The code for aligning the cell content can be given here. The first appearance of this code is relevant.

charoff

Gives the gap to the defined alignment code, which has appeared for the first time in char in pixels.

span

States how many columns are spanned in the normal table structure counting from the current column.

valign

Gives the vertical alignment within the column.

Value	Meaning
bottom	The content is aligned to the bottom.
top	The content is aligned to the top.

Table 2.11 *The value of valign in <col>*

width

Gives the entire width of the column in pixels or as a percentile value of the browser window width.

Example:

```
<table border=1 cols=2>
  <colgroup>
    <col ALIGN="right">
  </colgroup>
  <colgroup>
    <col ALIGN="center">
```

```
    <col ALIGN="center">
  </colgroup>
  <caption>Browser statistic</caption>
  <tr><th>Browser</th><th>Market share</th></tr>
  <tr><td>Microsoft Internet Explorer</td><td>60.4 %</td>
  </tr>
  <tr><td>Netscape Communicator</td><td>38.5 %</td></tr>
  <tr><td>Others</td><td>1.1 %</td></tr>
</table>
```

See:

`<caption>`, `<colgroup>`, `<thead>`, `<tbody>`, `<tfoot>`, `<table>`, `<th>`, `<td>`, `<tr>`

2.4.6   *<colgroup>*

Tag/Attribute	2.0	3.0	3.2	4.0	Internet Explorer	Netscape
`<colgroup>`				X	3.0AI	
`align`				X	4.0BI	
`bgcolor`					4.0	
`char`				X		
`charoff`				X		
`span`				X	3.0AI	
`valign`				X	4.0BI	
`width`				X	4.0BI	

This tag is used in the `<table>` ... `</table>` and contains only `<col>` tags. It enables formatting of the columns even before the data summarizing of the table.

align

Gives the horizontal alignment within the column group.

Value	Meaning
`center`	The content is aligned to the center.
`left`	The content is aligned to the left.
`right`	The content is aligned to the right.

Table 2.12 *The values for align in <colgroup>*

bgcolor

The background color of the column group is set here. RGB values and, for many browser, predefined color values (see Appendix B) are the standard.

char

The code for aligning the cell content can be given here. The first appearance of this code is relevant.

charoff

Gives the gap to the defined alignment code, which has appeared for the first time in char in pixels.

span

States how many columns are in the group without having to count them using <col>.

valign

Gives the vertical alignment within the row group.

Value	Meaning
bottom	The content is aligned to the bottom.
top	The content is aligned to the bottom.

Table 2.13 *The values for valign in <colgroup>*

width

Gives the whole width of the column in pixels or as percentile value of the browser window width.

Example:

```
<table border=1 cols=2>
  <colgroup>
    <col ALIGN="right">
  </colgroup>
  <colgroup>
    <col ALIGN="center">
    <col ALIGN="center">
  </colgroup>
  <caption>Browser statistic</caption>
  <tr><th>Browser</th><th>Market share</th></tr>
  <tr><td>Microsoft Internet Explorer</td><td>60.4 %</td>
  </tr>
  <tr><td>Netscape Communicator</td><td>38.5 %</td></tr>
  <tr><td>Others</td><td>1.1 %</td></tr>
</table>
```

See:

`<caption>`, `<col>`, `<thead>`, `<tbody>`, `<tfoot>`, `<table>`, `<th>`, `<td>`, `<tr>`

2.4.7 *<comment>*

Tag/Attribute	2.0	3.0	3.2	4.0	Internet Explorer	Netscape
`<comment>`					1.0	

The browser ignores passages, which are enclosed by `<comment>` ... `</comment>`

Example:

`This text <comment> </comment> does not appear on the screen.`

See:

`<!-- ... -->`

2.5 D

2.5.1 *<dd>*

Tag/Attribute	2.0	3.0	3.2	4.0	Internet Explorer	Netscape
`<dd>`	X	X	X	X	1.0	1.0
`clear`		X				
`no wrap`					4.0	

This tag is used within lists of definitions `<dl>` ... `</dl>` and includes a definition description. The text is generally indented on the left side.

clear

This attribute was supplemented to allow the user to work with images, which are moved left to right by the attribute `align` in `<img>`. It can be used when working with all objects, which are moved by `align`.

Value	Meaning
none	A normal word wrap is produced.
left	The line is wrapped and the next line should be inserted in such a way that the left border is free of images (or other objects).
right	The line is wrapped and the next line should be inserted in such a way that the right border is free of images (or other objects).
all	The line is wrapped and the next line should be inserted in such a way that all borders are free of images (or other objects).

Table 2.14 *The values for clear in <dd>*

no wrap

States whether the normal HTML word wrap rules are valid or whether these should be ignored.

Value	Meaning
false	The normal rules apply: text, which has come to the end of the line, will be automatically wrapped.
true	Text, which has come to the end of the line, will not be wrapped. Exceptions will only be made in the case of specified formatting (, <p>, etc)

Table 2.15 *The values for no wrap in <dd>*

Example:

```
<dl>
  <dt>Definition A</dt>
  <dd>Definition B is incorrect.</dd>
  <dt>Definition B</dt>
  <dd>Definition A is correct.</dd>
</dl>
```

See:

```
<dir>, <dl>, <dt>, <li>, <menu>, <ol>, <ul>
```

2.5.2   *<del>*

Tag/Attribute	2.0	3.0	3.2	4.0	Internet Explorer	Netscape
<del>		X		X	4.0	
cite				X		
datetime				X		

This deals with the deletion of text passages and other source codes without deleting them from the source text. As a time is given when the deletion takes place, some browsers can display the page in the same format as at a time selected by the user. Other browsers show deleted passages in a different color from the current passages and the remaining browsers show only the current status.

cite

Gives a URL, explaining why the deletion process was necessary.

datetime

Gives the date and time of the deletion. The value is given in the format `yyyy-mm-ddThh:mm:ssCET`.

Value	Description
yyyy	Year in four digits.
mm	Month in two digits. (01-12)
dd	Day in two digits. (01-31)
hh	Hour in two digits. (00-23)
mm	Minute in two digits. (00-59)
ss	Second in two digits. (00-59)

Table 2.16 *The values for datetime in <del>*

Example:

```
<del cite="http://www.berlin.de">Berlin Wall</del>
```

See:

```
<ins>
```

2.5.3   <dfn>

Tag/Attribute	2.0	3.0	3.2	4.0	Internet Explorer	Netscape
<dfn>	X	X	X	X	1.0	

Marks definitions and generally shows these in italics.

Example:

```
<dfn>
  When the cock crows on the manure, the weather changes
  or it stays as it is.
</dfn>
```

See:

```
<address>, <blockquote>, <center>, <cite>, <code>, <h1>,
<h2>, <h3>, <h4>, <h5>, <h6>, <marquee>, <multicol>, <p>,
<pre>
```

2.5.4   *<dir>*

Tag/Attribute	2.0	3.0	3.2	4.0	Internet Explorer	Netscape
`<dir>`	X	X	X	X	1.0	1.0
`compact`	X	X	X	X		
`type`						4.0

This tag produces a list of (generally) short entries. These are separated by `<li>`.

compact

This sole attribute states that at least one presentation should be selected, which saves space.

type

States which points should be used in the list.

Value	Meaning
`A`	A, B, C, D, ...
`a`	a, b, c, d, ...
`I`	I, II, III, IV, ...
`i`	i, ii, iii, iv, ...
`1`	1, 2, 3, 4, ...
`disc`	disc
`square`	square
`circle`	circle

Table 2.17   *The values for type in <dir>*

Example:

```
<dir>
  <li type="disc">disc
  <li type="circle">circle
  <li type="square">square
</dir>
```

See:

```
<dd>, <dl>, <dt>, <li>, <menu>, <ol>, <ul>
```

2.5.5   *<div>*

Tag/Attribute	2.0	3.0	3.2	4.0	Internet Explorer	Netscape
<div>		X	X	X	3.0A1	2.0
align		X	X	X	3.0A1	2.0
clear		X				
no wrap					4.0	

This text marks an excerpt in a text, which should begin with a word wrap and also end with a word wrap.

align

Gives the horizontal alignment of the excerpt.

Value	Meaning
center	The content is aligned in the center.
justify	The content is written in block capitals.
left	The content is aligned to the left.
right	The content is aligned to the right.

Table 2.18   *The values for align in <div>*

clear

This attribute was supplemented to ensure that the user can work with images, which are moved to the left or right by the attribute align in <img>. It can be used when working with all objects, which are moved by align.

Value	Meaning
none	A normal word wrap is produced.
left	The line is wrapped and the next line should be inserted in such a way that the left border is free of images (or other objects).
right	The line is wrapped and the next line should be inserted in such a way that the right border is free of images (or other objects).
all	The line is wrapped and the next line should be inserted in such a way that all borders are free of images (or other objects).

Table 2.19   *The values for clear in <div>*

no wrap

States whether the normal HTML word wrap rules are valid or whether these should be ignored.

Value	Meaning
false	The normal rules apply: text, which has come to the end of the line, is automatically wrapped.
true	Text, which has come to the end of the line, is not wrapped. Exceptions can only be made for specific formatting (` `, `<p>`, etc).

Table 2.20 *The values for no wrap in <div>*

Example:

```
<div>This is a complete sentence.</div>
```

2.5.6   <dl>

Tag/Attribute	2.0	3.0	3.2	4.0	Internet Explorer	Netscape
<dl>	X	X	X	X	1.0	1.0
clear		X				
compact	X	X	X	X	4.0B1	1.0

A list of definitions, containing such entries as `<dd>` and `<dt>` is produced here.

clear

This attribute was supplemented to ensure that the user can work with images which are moved to the left or right by the attribute `align` in `<img>`. It can be used when working with all objects, which are moved by `align`.

Value	Meaning
none	A normal word wrap is produced.
left	The line is wrapped and the next line should be inserted in such a way that the left border is free of images (or other objects).
right	The line is wrapped and the next line should be inserted in such a way that the right border is free of images (or other objects).
all	The line is wrapped and the next line should be inserted in such a way that all borders are free of images (or other objects).

Table 2.21 *The values for clear in <dl>*

compact

This sole attribute states that at least one presentation should be selected, which saves space.

Example:

```
<dl>
  <dt>Definition A</dt>
  <dd>Definition B is incorrect.</dd>
  <dt>Definition B</dt>
  <dd>Definition A is correct.</dd>
</dl>
```

See:

`<dd>`, `<dir>`, `<dt>`, `<li>`, `<menu>`, `<ol>`, `<ul>`

2.5.7   *<dt>*

Tag/Attribute	2.0	3.0	3.2	4.0	Internet Explorer	Netscape
`<dt>`	X	X	X	X	1.0	1.0
`clear`		X				
`no wrap`				4.0		

This tag stands for "definition term" and is used in definition lists `<dl>`.

clear

This attribute was supplemented to ensure that the user can work with images which are moved to the left or right by the attribute `align` in `<img>`. It can be used when working with all objects, which are moved by `align`.

Value	Meaning
`none`	A normal word wrap is produced.
`left`	The line is wrapped and the next line should be inserted in such a way that the left border is free of images (or other objects).
`right`	The line is wrapped and the next line should be inserted in such a way that the right border is free of images (or other objects).
`all`	The line is wrapped and the next line should be inserted in such a way that all borders are free of images (or other objects).

Table 2.22   *The values for clear in <dt>*

no wrap

States whether the normal HTML word wrap rules apply or whether these should be ignored.

Value	Meaning
false	The normal rules apply: text, which has come to the end of the line, is automatically wrapped.
true	Text, which has come to the end of the line, is not wrapped. Exceptions can only be made for specific formatting (` `, `<p>`, etc).

Table 2.23 *The values for no wrap in <dt>*

Example:

```
<dl>
  <dt>Definition A</dt>
  <dd>Definition B is incorrect.</dd>
  <dt>Definition B</dt>
  <dd>Definition A is correct.</dd>
</dl>
```

See:

`<dd>, <dir>, <dl>, <li>, <menu>, <ol>, <ul>`

2.6 E

2.6.1 *<em>*

Tag/Attribute	2.0	3.0	3.2	4.0	Internet Explorer	Netscape
`<em>`	X	X	X	X	1.0	1.0

This tag marks text which should be highlighted. This is usually presented in italics.

Example:

`<em>this text is highlighted,</em> but this is not.`

See:

`<abbr>, <b>, <big>, <blink>, <font>, <i>, <kbd>, <q>, <s>, <samp>, <small>, <strike>, <strong>, <sub>, <sup>, <tt>, <u>, <var>`

2.6.2   <embed>

Tag/Attribute	2.0	3.0	3.2	4.0	Internet Explorer	Netscape
<embed>					3.0B2	1.1
height					3.0B2	1.1
src					3.0B2	1.1
width					3.0B2	1.1

This tag is used to integrate plug-in data into the browser. The above-mentioned attribute is called up directly by the browser and all remaining attributes are passed on unaltered to the plug-in.

height

Gives the height of the plug-in in pixels or as a percentile value of the height of the browser window.

src

Gives the URL of the plug-in data to be displayed.

width

Gives the width of the plug-in in pixels or as a percentile value of the height of the browser window.

Example:

```
<embed src="a_song.mid" controls>
  <noembed>
    Your browser does not support the integration of the
    <a HREF="a_song.mid">song</a>.
  </noembed>
</embed>
```

See:

```
<applet>, <iframe>, <noembed>, <noscript>, <param>,
<script>
```

2.7 F

2.7.1 *<fieldset>*

Tag/Attribute	2.0	3.0	3.2	4.0	Internet Explorer	Netscape
`<fieldset>`				X	4.0B2	
`align`					4.0	

Summarizes the elements of the entry from forms to groups .

align

Gives the horizontal alignment within the group.

Value	Meaning
`center`	The content is aligned in the center.
`left`	The content is aligned to the left.
`right`	The content is aligned to the right.

Table 2.24 *The values for align in <fieldset>*

Example:

```
<form>
  <fieldset>
    <legend accesskey="b" tabindex=1>
     Order newsletter
    </legend>
    <label accesskey="j">
      <input type="radio" name=news value="yes">yes
    </label><br>
    <label accesskey="n">
      <input type="radio" name=news value="no">no
    </label><br>
  </fieldset>
</form>
```

TAKE THHAT!

Result:

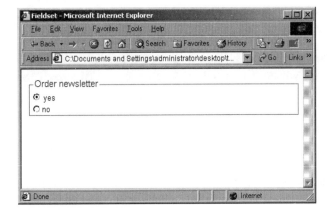

Figure 2.1 *A form area*

See:

`<button>`, `<form>`, `<input>`, `<keygen>`, `<label>`, `<legend>`, `<optgroup>`, `<option>`, `<select>`, `<textarea>`

2.7.2 `<font>`

Tag/Attribute	2.0	3.0	3.2	4.0	Internet Explorer	Netscape
`<font>`			X	X	1.0	1.0
color			X	X	1.0	2.0
face				X	1.0	3.0B5
point-size						4.0B5
size			X	X	1.0	1.0

This tag is one of the most powerful means for structuring typeface in the HTML 4. The attributes affect the typeface and the point size.

color

The color of the text is set here. RGB values and, for many browsers, predefined color values (see Appendix B) are the standard.

face

A list of the names of typeface separated by commas. When the appropriate typeface has been found (and installed in the system) it will be used as standard typeface for the text contained in this tag.

point size

Gives the point size of the typeface and is an alternative to `size`.

size

Represents the point size. Applicable values are `1` to `7`. If precedence is given to the value + or - the size will be calculated relative to the actual size of the typeface.

Example:

```
<font face="arial" size=+2>
```

See:

`<abbr>`, `<b>`, `<big>`, `<blink>`, `<em>`, `<i>`, `<kbd>`, `<q>`, `<s>`, `<samp>`, `<small>`, `<strike>`, `<strong>`, `<sub>`, `<sup>`, `<tt>`, `<u>`, `<var>`

2.7.3 *<form>*

Tag/Attribute	2.0	3.0	3.2	4.0	Internet Explorer	Netscape
`<form>`	X	X	X	X	1.0	1.0
`accept`				X		
`accept-charset`				X		
`action`	X	X	X	X	1.0	1.0
`autocomplete`					5.0	
`enctype`	X	X	X	X	1.0	1.0
`method`	X	X	X	X	1.0	1.0
`name`				X	3.0B1	2.0
`target`				X	3.0A1	2.0

A form is set out here. All elements of the form (for example `<input>`) are enclosed by `<form> ... </form>`.

accept

States which MIME formats may send the form to ensure that the server reacts correctly to it. These formats are separated by commas.

accept charset

Gives the font for dispatch of the form. These are separated by commas.

action

Gives the address of the typeface or server, which should evaluate the form data.

autocomplete

Switches the auto completion function on (on) or off (off).

enctype

Gives the MIME media type in which the data should be coded during the dispatch process.

method

States how the form should send the data:

Value	Meaning
post	The data is sent as a separate data flow direct to the typeface.
get	The data is attached to the URL here and submitted with the target type-face.

Table 2.25 *The values for method in <form>*

name

States the name of the form for the purpose of addressing it via typeface and if necessary to change it.

target

Gives the target frame, in which the resulting data should be displayed following dispatch of the form data.

Example:

```
<form method="post" action="mailto:my@address.com">
  <fieldset>
    <legend accesskey="b" tabindex=1>
    Order newsletter </legend>
    <label accesskey="j" name="yes">
      <input type="radio" name=news value="yes">yes
    </label><br>
    <label accesskey="n" name="no">
      <input type="radio" name=news value="no">no
    </label><br>
  </fieldset>
  <input type="submit" value="Send form">
  <input type="reset" value="Delete form">
</form>
```

See:

```
<button>, <fieldset>, <input>, <keygen>, <label>,
<legend>, <optgroup>, <option>, <select>, <textarea>
```

2.7.4   <frame>

Tag/Attribute	2.0	3.0	3.2	4.0	Internet Explorer	Netscape
`<frame>`				X	3.0AI	2.0
`application`					5.0	
`bordercolor`					4.0B2	3.0B5
`frameborder`				X	3.0AI	3.0B5
`longdesc`				X		
`marginheight`				X	3.0AI	2.0
`marginwidth`				X	3.0AI	2.0
`name`				X	3.0AI	2.0
`noresize`				X	3.0AI	2.0
`scrolling`				X	3.0AI	2.0
`src`				X	3.0AI	2.0

This tag produces a frame within `<frameset> ... </frameset>`. The attributes of this tag affect the single frame.

application

States whether the content of the frame is an HTA (HTML application) and therefore not subject to the Internet Explorer safety regulations.

Value	Meaning
`no`	The safety regulations remain unaltered.
`yes`	The frame content is completely reliable.

Table 2.26   *The values for application in <frame>*

bordercolor

The color of the border is set here. RGB values and, for many browsers, predefined color values (see Appendix B) are the standard. Values set by `<frameset>` can be overwritten.

frameborder

States whether a border should be drawn around the frame. (This is, however, only switched off if all frames, which are on the border, have turned it off.)

Value	Meaning
0	The border is turned off. (Netscape)
1	The border is turned on. (Netscape)
no	The border is turned off. (Microsoft)
yes	The border is turned on. (Microsoft)

Table 2.27 *The value of the attribute frame border in <frame>*

longdesc

Gives an address which delivers a longer description of the border content.

marginheight

Gives the upper and lower gap from the border of the frame to the text. The value must be greater than 0 and is given in pixels.

marginwidth

Gives the left and right gap from the border of the frame to the text. The value must be greater than 0 and is given in pixels.

name

Gives the frame a name with which other tags can address it using their `target` attributes.

noresize

This sole attribute prohibits the change of the size of the frame.

scrolling

States whether the scroll bar should be displayed.

Value	Meaning
auto	Scroll bar should appear as necessary.
no	Scroll bar should never appear.
yes	Scroll bar should always appear.

Table 2.28 *The values for scrolling in <frame>*

src

Gives the URL for the page, which should be represented in the frame.

Example:

```
<html>
  <head>
    <title>A frame example</title>
  </head>
```

```
<frameset rows=20%,60%,20%>
  <frame src="a.htm" name="above">
  <frameset cols=50%,50%>
    <frame src="b.htm" name="left in the middle">
    <frame src="c.htm" name="right in the middle">
  </frameset>
  <frame src="d.htm" name="down">
</frameset>
<noframes>
  <head>
    <title>A frame example (unfortunately your
browser is too old)</title>
  </head>
  <body>
    <center>
      WARNING!<P>
      YOU ARE USING A BROWSER, WHICH DOES NOT SUPPORT
      FRAMES. PLEASE CLICK
      <a href="a.htm">HERE</a>, TO OBTAIN
A VERSION WITH NO FRAMES!<p>
    </center>
  </body>
</noframes>
</html>
```

See:

```
<frameset>, <noframes>
```

2.7.5   *<frameset>*

Tag/Attribute	2.0	3.0	3.2	4.0	Internet Explorer	Netscape
<frameset>				X	3.0A1	2.0
border					4.0B1	3.0B5
bordercolor					4.0B2	3.0B5
cols				X	3.0A1	2.0
frameborder					3.0A1	3.0B5
framespacing					3.0A1	
rows				X	3.0A1	2.0

This tag states that this page should produce a border. It replaces the <body> tag and contains <frame> tags as well as possible additional <frameset> instructions.

frameset

This tag is defined in the outer `<frameset>` tag and gives the border strength for all frames in pixels. If the value is `0`, a `frameborder=no` will mandatorily appear in all frames.

bordercolor

The color of the frame border is set here. RGB values and, for many browsers, predefined color values (see Appendix B) are the standard.

cols

Gives the width of the individual columns separated by commas.

Values	Meaning
positive, whole numbers	Width in pixels
percentile value	Percentile width of the current frames
`*`, `2*`, etc	Parts of the available remaining width

Table 2.29 *The values for cols in <frameset>*

frameborder

States whether a border should be drawn around the frame. (This is only switched off if all frames, which are on the border, have turned it off.)

Value	Meaning
`0`	The border is turned off. (Netscape)
`1`	The border is turned on. (Netscape)
`no`	The border is turned off. (Microsoft)
`yes`	The border is turned on. (Microsoft)

Table 2.30 *The values of the attribute frameborder in <frame>*

framespacing

Gives the width of the space between single frames in pixels.

rows

Gives the height of the single rows separated by commas.

Values	Meaning
positive, whole numbers	Width in pixels.
percentile value	Percentile width of the current frame.
, 2, etc	Parts of the available remaining width.

Table 2.31 *The values of rows in <frameset>*

Example:

```
<html>
  <head>
    <title>A frame example</title>
  </head>
  <frameset rows=20%,60%,20%>
    <frame src="a.htm" name="above">
    <frameset cols=50%,50%>
      <frame src="b.htm" name="left in the middle">
      <frame src="c.htm" name="right in the middle">
    </frameset>
    <frame src="d.htm" name="below">
  </frameset>
  <noframes>
    <head>
      <title>A frame example (your browser is
unfortunately too old)</title>
    </head>
    <body>
      <center>
        WARNING!<P>
        YOU ARE USING A BROWSER, WHICH DOES NOT SUPPORT
FRAMES. CLICK
        <a href="a.htm">HERE</a>, TO OBTAIN
A VERSION WITH NO FRAMES!<p>
      </center>
    </body>
  </noframes>
</html>
```

See:

<body>, <head>, <html>, <frame>, <noframes>

TAKE THHAT!

2

2.8.1 <h1> ... <h6>

Tag/Attribute	2.0	3.0	3.2	4.0	Internet Explorer	Netscape
`<h1> ... <h6>`	X	X	X	X	1.0	1.0
`align`		X	X	X	1.0	1.0
`clear`		X				

A signature is produced here. `<h1>` produces a first grade signature and `<h6>` a signature of the 6th degree.

align

Gives the horizontal alignment of the signature.

Value	Meaning
`center`	The signature is aligned in the center.
`left`	The signature is aligned to the left.
`right`	The signature is aligned to the right.

Table 2.32 *The values for align in <h1> ... <h6>*

clear

This attribute was supplemented to be able to work with images, which are moved left or right by the attribute `align` in `<img>`. It can be used when working with all objects, which are moved by `align`.

Value	Meaning
`none`	A normal word wrap is produced.
`left`	The line is wrapped and the next line should be inserted in such a way that the left border is free of images (or other objects).
`right`	The line is wrapped and the next line should be inserted in such a way that the right border is free of images (or other objects).
`all`	The line is wrapped and the next line should be inserted in such a way that all borders are free of images (or other objects).

Table 2.33 *The values for* `clear` *in* `<h1> ... <h6>`

Example:

```
<h1>1 Introduction</h1>
<h2>1.1 What is HTML?</h2>
<h2>1.2 Requirements</h2>
<h3>1.2.1 Text editor</h3>
<h3>1.2.2 Browser</h3>
<h2>1.3 HTML basics</h2>
<h3>1.3.1 Hello World! </h3>
<h3>1.3.2 Tags</h3>
<h3>1.3.3 Head and body</h3>
<h3>1.3.4 Attributes</h3>
```

Result:

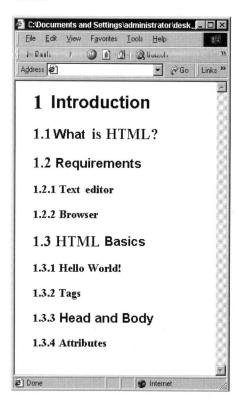

Figure 2.2 *Does this strike you as familiar?*

See:

```
<address>, <blockquote>, <center>, <cite>, <code>, <dfn>,
<marquee>, <multicol>, <p>, <pre>
```

2.8.2   <head>

Tag/Attribute	2.0	3.0	3.2	4.0	Internet Explorer	Netscape
<head>	X	X	X	X	1.0	1.0
profile				X		

This tag marks the head of an HTML row. The area between <head> ... </head> does not contain any real document information, solely information on the content of the document.

profile

Gives a list of URLs to META data profiles, these are separated by spaces.

Example:

```
<html>
  <head>
    <!—Information on the content is given here.-->
  </head>
  <body>
    The content is given here.
  </body>
</html>
```

See:

<body>, <html>, <frameset>

2.8.3   <hr>

Tag/Attribute	2.0	3.0	3.2	4.0	Internet Explorer	Netscape
<hr>	X	X	X	X	1.0	1.0
align			X	X	1.0	1.0
color					3.0A1	
noshade			X	X	1.0	1.0
size			X	X	1.0	1.0
width			X	X	1.0	1.0

Represents a horizontal dividing line on the screen.

align

Gives the horizontal alignment of the line.

Value	Meaning
center	The line is aligned to the center
left	The line is aligned to the left.
right	The line is aligned to the right.

Table 2.34 *The values for align in <hr>*

color

The color of the line is set here. RGB values and, for many browsers, predefined color values (see Appendix B) are the standard.

noshade

This sole attribute states that the line should be represented in a single color and not in 3D optics.

size

Gives the width of the line in pixels.

width

Gives the width of the line in pixels or relative to the browser width.

Example:

```
<hr width=50%>
```

2.8.4   <html>

Tag/Attribute	2.0	3.0	3.2	4.0	Internet Explorer	Netscape
<html>	X	X	X	X	1.0	1.0

This tag has the highest hierarchical level. All other tags can be found in <html> ... </html>. The function of this tag is therefore to highlight the complete HTML code.

Example:

```
<html>
  <head>
    <!—Content information can be found here.-->
  </head>
  <body>
    The content is here.
  </body>
</html>
```

See:

`<body>, <head>, <frameset>`

2.9.1   *<i>*

Tag/Attribute	2.0	3.0	3.2	4.0	Internet Explorer	Netscape
`<i>`	X	X	X	X	1.0	1.0

This tag marks text which can be presented in italics.

Example:

`<i>This text is printed in italics,</i> but this is not.`

See:

`<abbr>, <b>, <big>, <blink>, <em>, <font>, <kbd>, <q>, <s>, <samp>, <small>, <strike>, <strong>, <sub>, <sup>, <tt>, <u>, <var>`

2.9.2   *<iframe>*

Tag/Attribute	2.0	3.0	3.2	4.0	Internet Explorer	Netscape
`<iframe>`				X	3.0B2	
`align`				X	3.0B2	
`application`					5.0	
`frameborder`				X	3.0B2	
`height`				X	3.0B2	
`hspace`					3.0B2	
`longdesc`				X		
`marginheight`				X	3.0B2	
`marginwidth`				X	3.0B2	
`name`				X	3.0B2	
`scrolling`				X	3.0B2	
`src`				X	3.0B2	
`vspace`					3.0B2	
`width`				X	3.0B2	

This frame is called inline-frame and differs from `<frame>` in that it must not be integrated into a `<frameset>` structure. An Internet page is inserted in a set area of the page and, with regard to measurements, is handled the same way as an image inserted using `<img>`.

align

Gives the alignment of the text, which dictates the alignment of the frame.

Value	Meaning
middle	The text is aligned vertically in the middle.
left	The text is aligned to the left.
right	The text is aligned to the right.
top	The text is aligned to the top.
bottom	The text is aligned to the bottom.

Table 2.35 *The values for align in <iframe>*

application

States whether the frame content is an HTA (HTML application) and therefore not subject to Internet Explorer safety regulations.

Value	Meaning
no	The safety regulations remain unaltered.
yes	The frame content is completely reliable.

Table 2.36 *The values for application in <iframe>*

frameborder

States whether a border should be drawn around the frame.

Value	Meaning
0	The border is switched off.
1	The border is switched on.

Table 2.37 *The values of the attribute frameborder in <iframe>*

height

Gives the height of the border in pixels.

hspace

Gives the left and right space from the border to all other HTML components in pixels.

longdesc

Gives an address, which provides a longer description of the border content.

marginheight

Gives the upper and lower space from the frame border to the text. The value must be greater than 0 and is given in pixels.

marginwidth

Gives the left and right space from the frame border to the text. The value must be greater than 0 and is given in pixels.

name

Gives the frame a name, with which other tags can address it using their `target` attribute.

scrolling

States whether the scroll bar should be displayed.

Value	Meaning
auto	Scroll bar appears as necessary.
no	Scroll bar should never appear.
yes	Scroll bar should always appear.

Table 2.38 *The values for scrolling in <iframe>*

src

Gives the URL of the page, which should be presented in the frame.

vspace

Gives the upper and lower space from the border to all other HTML components in pixels.

width

Gives the width of the frame in pixels.

Example:

```
<iframe src="one_page.htm" width="400" height="300">
  Your browser does not support inline frames.
  Please click <a href="a_page.htm">hier</a>.<br>
</iframe>
```

See:

`<applet>`, `<embed>`, `<noembed>`, `<noscript>`, `<param>`, `<script>`

2.9.3   <img>

Tag/Attribute	2.0	3.0	3.2	4.0	Internet Explorer	Netscape
`<img>`	X	X	X	X	1.0	1.0
`align`	X	X	X	X	1.0	1.0
`alt`	X	X	X	X	1.0	1.0
`border`			X	X	1.0	1.0
`controls`					2.0	
`dynsrc`					2.0	
`height`		X	X	X	1.0	1.0
`hspace`			X	X	1.0	1.0
`ismap`	X	X	X	X	1.0	1.0
`longdesc`				X		
`loop`					2.0	
`lowsrc`					4.0B1	1.0
`name`				X	4.0	3.0
`src`	X	X	X	X	1.0	1.0
`start`					2.0	
`suppress`						4.0
`usemap`			X	X	1.0	2.0
`vrml`					2.0	
`vspace`			X	X	1.0	1.0
`width`		X	X	X	1.0	1.0

This tag is the standard variation for inserting pictures, graphics and videos into an HTML page.

align

Gives the alignment of the text, which dictates the alignment of the picture.

Value	Meaning
`middle`	The text is aligned vertically in the middle.
`left`	The text is aligned to the left.
`right`	The text is aligned to the right.
`top`	The text is aligned to the top.
`bottom`	The text is aligned to the bottom.

Table 2.39   *The values for align in <img>*

alt

The value of this attribute is given when the browser does not recognize `<img>`. This is true for old text browsers for example.

border

Gives the width of the border, which is shown around an image, when it is used as an anchor for a link. It contains the colors, which would have a normal text link.

controls

This sole attribute states whether the page reader should obtain the controls for the video process or for other data sources, defined by `dynsrc`.

dynsrc

This attribute gives the address of a video, which should be played using this tag.

height

Gives the height of the image in pixels or as a percentile value of the height of the browser window.

hspace

Gives the left and right space from the image to all other HTML components in pixels.

ismap

This sole attribute states that hot areas have been defined for this image, which can be activated by a mouse click.

longdesc

Gives an address, which provides a longer description of the image content.

loop

States how often a video should be repeated.

lowsrc

Gives the URL an image with lower quality, which is loaded, before the image from src is loaded with a higher resolution.

name

Gives a name for the image, which will be used later for addressing via script languages.

src

Gives the URL of an image, which should be displayed here.

start

This attribute is used in connection with `dynsrc` and states when the video should be started.

Value	Meaning
fileopen	The video is played as soon as it has been completely downloaded.
mou- seover	The video is played when it has been completely downloaded as well as when the mouse has been moved over it.

Table 2.40 *The values for start in <img>*

suppress

This attribute states whether the appearance of an icon, which is displayed when the image has not yet been completely downloaded, should be suppressed.

Value	Meaning
false	The normal icon remains.
true	Supresses the icon.

Table 2.41 *The values for suppress in <img>*

usemap

Gives the address to the image map specifications for the client.

vrml

Gives a URL to a VRML world and starts a VRML plugin, if installed.

vspace

Gives the upper and lower space from the border to all other HTML components in pixels.

width

Gives the width of the image in pixels or as a percentile value of the width of the browser window.

Example:

```
<img src="an_image.jpg" alt="My Portrait">
<img src="a_film.jpg" alt="A film should play here." dyn-
src="a_film.avi">
```

See:

```
<area>, <bgsound>, <map>, <object>
```

2.9.4   <ins>

Tag/Attribute	2.0	3.0	3.2	4.0	Internet Explorer	Netscape
`<ins>`		X		X	4.0	
`cite`				X		
`datetime`						

This deals with the insertion of text passages and other source codes without losing the source text version. As a time is given when the insertion takes place, some browsers can display the page in the same format as at a time selected by the user. Other browsers show inserted passages in a different color from the old passages and the remaining browsers show only the current status.

cite

Gives a URL which explains why the insertion was necessary.

datetime

Gives the date and the time of the insertion. The value is given in the format `yyyy-mm-ddThh:mm:ssCET`.

Value	Description
`yyyy`	Year in four digits
`mm`	Month in two digits (`01-12`)
`dd`	Day in two digits (`01-31`)
`hh`	Hour in two digits (`00-23`)
`mm`	Minutes in two digits (`00-59`)
`ss`	Seconds in two digits (`00-59`)

Table 2.42   *The values for datetime in <ins>*

Example:

`Berlin <ins cite="http://www.berlin.de">(Capital)</ins>`

See:

`<del>`

Tag/Attribute	2.0	3.0	3.2	4.0	Internet Explorer	Netscape
\<input type="button"\>				X	3.0BI	I.0
accesskey				X	4.0BI	
disabled				X	4.0BI	
height						4.0B2
name				X	3.0BI	I.0
tabindex				X	4.0BI	
value				X	3.0BI	I.0
width						4.0B2

This tag is used in forms, which were produced with \<form\> ... \</form\>. It produces a button using the value button for the attribute type.

accesskey

You can define a shortcut key to access the form element using accesskey. Assign the attribute a single letter and it will be executed when you hit this key with the appropriate shortcut key. This key is dependent on the browser and operational system.

disabled

This sole attribute ensures that the form element is registered as inactive and prevents the element from functioning.

height

Gives the height of the button in pixels.

name

Gives the name of the form element to enable identification via scripts. The value of the attribute is also given when the form is evaluated.

tabindex

Gives the tab index for the form element. Positive values stand for the position of the element in the list of objects activated by [⇥] . Negative values mean that the element does not appear in the tab index.

value

Gives the return value to the script in case this form element was activated.

width

Gives the width of the button in pixels.

2

TAKE THHAT!

See:

`<button>`, `<fieldset>`, `<form>`, `<keygen>`, `<label>`, `<legend>`, `<optgroup>`, `<option>`, `<select>`, `<textarea>`

Tag/Attribute	2.0	3.0	3.2	4.0	Internet Explorer	Netscape
`<input type="check- box">`	X	X	X	X	1.0	1.0
`accesskey`				X	4.0B1	
`checked`	X	X	X	X	1.0	1.0
`disabled`		X		X	4.0B1	
`name`	X	X	X	X	1.0	1.0
`tabindex`				X	4.0B1	
`value`	X	X	X	X	1.0	1.0

This tag is used in forms produced with `<form>` ... `</form>`. It produces a checkbox with the value `checkbox` for the attribute `type`.

accesskey

You can define a shortcut key to access the form element using `accesskey`. Assign the attribute a single letter and it will be executed when you hit this key with the appropriate shortcut key. This key is dependent on the browser and operational system.

checked

This sole attribute states that the form element in the standard form setting should be activated.

disabled

This sole attribute ensures that the form element is registered as inactive and prevents the element from functioning.

name

Gives the name of the form element to enable identification via scripts. The value of the attribute is also given when the form is evaluated.

tabindex

Gives the tab index for the form element. Positive values stand for the position of the element in the list of objects activated by ⇥ . Negative values mean that the element does not appear in the tab index.

value

Gives the return value to the script in case this form element was activated.

See:

```
<button>, <fieldset>, <form>, <keygen>, <label>, <legend>,
<optgroup>, <option>, <select>, <textarea>
```

Tag/Attribute	2.0	3.0	3.2	4.0	Internet Explorer	Netscape
`<input type="file">`		X	X	X	4.0B2	2.0
`accept`				X		
`accesskey`				X	4.0B2	
`disabled`		X		X	4.0B2	
`name`		X	X	X	4.0B2	2.0
`read only`					4.0B2	
`tabindex`				X		
`value`		X	X	X		

This tag is used in forms produced with `<form>` ... `</form>`. It produces a file selection field `file` for the attribute `type`.

accept

States which MIME formats may send the form to ensure that the script or the server react correctly to it. These formats are separated by commas.

accesskey

You can define a shortcut key to access the form element using `accesskey`. Assign the attribute a single letter and it will be executed when you hit this key with the appropriate shortcut key. This key is dependent on the browser and operational system.

disabled

This sole attribute ensures that the form element is registered as inactive and prevents the button from functioning.

name

Gives the name of the form element to enable identification via scripts. The value of the attribute is also given when the form is evaluated.

read only

This sole attribute states that the content of this form element may not be changed by the reader.

tabindex

Gives the tab index for the form element. Positive values stand for the position of the element in the list of objects activated by ⇥ . Negative values mean that the element does not appear in the tab index.

value

Gives the return value to the script (i.e. file name).

See:

`<button>`, `<fieldset>`, `<form>`, `<keygen>`, `<label>`, `<legend>`, `<opt-group>`, `<option>`, `<select>`, `<textarea>`

Tag/Attribute	2.0	3.0	3.2	4.0	Internet Explorer	Netscape
`<input type="hidden">`	X	X	X	X	1.0	1.0
name	X	X	X	X	1.0	1.0
value	X	X	X	X	1.0	1.0

This tag is used in forms produced by `<form>` ... `</form>`. It produces a hidden field with the value `hidden` for the attribute `type`. The reader has no influence over this field but can interact with the script.

name

Gives the name of the form element to enable identification via scripts. The value of the attribute is also given when the form is evaluated.

value

Gives the return value to the script.

See:

`<button>`, `<fieldset>`, `<form>`, `<keygen>`, `<label>`, `<legend>`, `<optgroup>`, `<option>`, `<select>`, `<textarea>`

Tag/Attribute	2.0	3.0	3.2	4.0	Internet Explorer	Netscape
`<input type="image">`	X	X	X	X	1.0	1.0
`accesskey`				X	4.0B1	
`align`	X	X	X	X	1.0	1.0
`alt`				X	4.0B2	4.0
`border`						1.0
`disabled`		X		X	4.0B2	
`height`					4.0B1	1.1
`ismap`				X		
`name`	X	X	X	X	1.0	1.0
`src`	X	X	X	X	1.0	1.0
`tabindex`				X	4.0B1	
`usemap`				X		2.0
`value`	X	X	X	X		
`width`					4.0B1	1.1

This tag is used in forms produced by `<form>` ... `</form>`. It produces an image with the value `image` for the attribute `type`. When the reader clicks on the image form data are sent. It works in the same way as `type=submit`, but also sends the coordinates to the script, which was clicked on in the image.

accesskey

You can define a shortcut key to access the form element using `accesskey`. Assign the attribute a single letter and it will be executed when you hit this key with the appropriate shortcut key. This key is dependent on the browser and operational system.

align

Gives the alignment of the text, which also dictates the alignment for the image.

Value	Meaning
`middle`	The text is aligned vertically in the middle.
`left`	The text is aligned to the left.
`right`	The text is aligned to the right.
`top`	The text is aligned to the top.
`bottom`	The text is aligned to the bottom.

Table 2.43 *The values for align in <input type="image">*

alt

The value of this attribute is given when the browser can not display images. This is true for old text browsers for example.

border

Gives the width of the border which is shown around an image. It contains the color which a normal text link would have.

disabled

This sole attribute ensures that the form element is registered as inactive and prevents the element from functioning.

height

Gives the height of the image in pixels.

ismap

This sole attribute states that hot areas were defined for this image. These hot areas can be activated by a mouse click.

name

Gives the name of the form element to enable identification via scripts. The value of the attribute is also given when the form is evaluated.

src

Gives the URL for an image which should be shown here.

tabindex

Gives the tab index for the form element. Positive values stand for the position of the element in the list of objects activated by ⇄ . Negative values mean that the element does not appear in the tab index.

usemap

Gives the address to the map specifications for the client.

value

Gives the return value to the script in case this form element is activated.

width

Gives the width of the image in pixels.

See:

```
<button>, <fieldset>, <form>, <keygen>, <label>, <legend>,
<optgroup>, <option>, <select>, <textarea>
```

Tag/Attribute	2.0	3.0	3.2	4.0	Internet Explorer	Netscape
`<input type="password">`	X	X	X	X	1.0	1.0
`accesskey`				X	4.0B1	
`autocomplete`					5.0	
`disabled`		X		X	4.0B1	
`name`	X	X	X	X	1.0	1.0
`read only`				X	4.0B1	
`tabindex`				X	4.0B1	
`value`	X	X	X	X	1.0	1.0
`vcard_name`					5.0	

This tag is used in forms produced by `<form>` ... `</form>`. It produces a password entry line with the value `password` for the attribute `type`.

accesskey

You can define a shortcut key to access the form element using `accesskey`. Assign the attribute a single letter and it will be executed when you hit this key with the appropriate shortcut key. This key is dependent on the browser and operational system.

autocomplete

Switches the auto completion function on (`on`) or off (`off`).

disabled

This sole attribute ensures that the form element is registered as inactive and prevents the element from functioning.

name

Gives the name of the form element to enable identification via scripts. The value of the attribute is also given when the form is evaluated.

read only

This sole attribute states that the content of this form element may not be changed by the reader.

tabindex

Gives the tab index for the form element. Positive values stand for the position of the element in the list of objects activated by $\boxed{\leftrightarrows}$. Negative values mean that the element does not appear in the tab index.

value

Gives the return value to the script.

vcard_name

Gives the field name of the personal Microsoft visiting card (vcard). The value of the card should be preset. The content of this field is forwarded to the recipient of the form data, when the form has been sent out.

Value	Meaning
vCard.Business.City	Business:city
vCard.Business.Country	Business:country
vCard.Business.Fax	Business.fax
vCard.Business.Phone	Business:phone
vCard.Business.State	Business:state
vCard.Business.StreetAddress	Business:street address
vCard.Business.URL	Business: URL
vCard.Business.ZipCode	Business:zip code
vCard.Cellular	Cellular
vCard.Company	Company
vCard.Department	Department
vCard.DisplayName	Display name
vCard.Email	E-mail
vCard.First Name	First name
vCard.Gender	Gender
vCard.Home.City	Home:city
vCard.Home.Country	Home:country
vCard.Home.Fax	Home:fax
vCard.Home.Phone	Home:phone
vCard.Home.State	Home:state
vCard.Home.StreetAddress	Home:street address
vCard.Home.ZipCode	Home:zip code
vCard.Homepage	Homepage
vCard.JobTitle	Job title
vCard.Last Name	Last name
vCard.Middle Name	Middle name
vCard.Notes	Notes
vCard.Office	Office
vCard.Pager	Pager

Table 2.44 *Values for vcard_name in <input type="password">*

See:

`<button>`, `<fieldset>`, `<form>`, `<keygen>`, `<label>`, `<legend>`, `<opt-group>`, `<option>`, `<select>`, `<textarea>`

Tag/Attribute	2.0	3.0	3.2	4.0	Internet Explorer	Netscape
`<input type="radio">`	X	X	X	X	I.0	I.0
`accesskey`				X	4.0BI	
`checked`	X	X	X	X	I.0	I.0
`disabled`		X		X	4.0BI	
`name`	X	X	X	X	I.0	I.0
`tabindex`				X	4.0BI	
`value`	X	X	X	X	I.0	I.0

This tag is used in forms produced with `<form>` ... `</form>`. It produces a radio button with the value `radio` for the attribute `type`.

accesskey

You can define a shortcut key to access the form element using `accesskey`. Assign the attribute a single letter and it will be executed when you hit this key with the appropriate shortcut key. This key is dependent on the browser and operational system.

checked

This sole states that the form element in the standard form setting should be activated.

disabled

This sole attribute ensures that the form element is registered as inactive and prevents the element from functioning.

name

Gives the name of the form element to ensure that it can be identified by scripts. The value of the attribute is also stated in the form evaluation.

tabindex

Gives the tab index for the form element. Positive values stand for the position of the element in the list of objects activated by ⇥ . Negative values mean that the element does not appear in the tab-index.

value

Gives the return value to the script in case this form element was activated.

```
<button>, <fieldset>, <form>, <keygen>, <label>, <legend>,
<optgroup>, <option>, <select>, <textarea>
```

Tag/Attribute	2.0	3.0	3.2	4.0	Internet Explorer	Netscape
`<input type="reset">`	X	X	X	X	1.0	1.0
`accesskey`				X	4.0B1	
`disabled`		X		X	4.0B1	
`height`						4.0B2
`tabindex`				X	4.0B1	
`value`	X	X	X	X	1.0	1.0
`width`						4.0B2

This tag is used in forms produced by `<form>` ... `</form>`. It produces a button, which can delete the form, with the value `reset` for the attribute `type`.

accesskey

You can define a shortcut key to access the form element using `accesskey`. Assign the attribute a single letter and it will be executed when you hit this key with the appropriate shortcut key. This key is dependent on the browser and operational system.

disabled

This sole attribute ensures that the form element is registered as inactive and prevents the element from functioning.

height

Gives the height of the button in pixels.

tabindex

Gives the tab index for the form element. Positive values stand for the position of the element in the list of objects activated by ⬚ . Negative values mean that the element does not appear in the tab-index.

value

Gives the return value to the script in case this form element was activated.

width

Gives the width of the button in pixels.

See:

```
<button>, <fieldset>, <form>, <keygen>, <label>, <legend>,
<optgroup>, <option>, <select>, <textarea>
```

TAKE THHAT!

Tag/Attribute	2.0	3.0	3.2	4.0	Internet Explorer	Netscape
`<input type = "submit">`	X	X	X	X	1.0	1.0
`accesskey`				X	4.0B1	
`disabled`		X		X	4.0B1	
`height`						4.0B2
`name`	X	X	X	X	1.0	1.0
`tabindex`				X	4.0B1	
`value`	X	X	X	X	1.0	1.0
`width`						4.0B2

This tag is used in forms produced by `<form> ... </form>`. It produces a button, which sends the form content, with the value `submit` for the attribute `type`.

accesskey

You can define a shortcut key to access the form element using `accesskey`. Assign the attribute a single letter and it will be executed when you hit this key with the appropriate shortcut key. This key is dependent on the browser and operational system.

disabled

This sole attribute ensures that the form element is registered as inactive and prevents the element from functioning.

height

Gives the height of the button in pixels.

name

Gives the name of the form element to ensure that it can be identified by scripts. The value of the attribute is also given in the evaluation of the form.

tabindex

Gives the tab index for the form element. Positive values stand for the position of the element in the list of objects activated by ⬒ . Negative values mean that the element does not appear in the tab-index.

value

Gives the return value to the script in case this form element was activated.

width

Gives the width of the button in pixels.

See:

`<button>`, `<fieldset>`, `<form>`, `<keygen>`, `<label>`, `<legend>`, `<optgroup>`, `<option>`, `<select>`, `<textarea>`

Tag/Attribute	2.0	3.0	3.2	4.0	Internet Explorer	Netscape
`<input type ="text">`	X	X	X	X	1.0	1.0
`accesskey`				X	4.0B1	
`autocomplete`					5.0	
`disabled`		X		X	4.0B1	
`maxlength`	X	X	X	X	1.0	1.0
`name`	X	X	X	X	1.0	1.0
`readonly`				X	4.0B1	
`size`	X	X	X	X	1.0	1.0
`tabindex`				X	4.0B1	
`value`	X	X	X	X	1.0	1.0
`vcard_name`					5.0	

This tag is used in forms produced by `<form>` ... `</form>`. It produces a text entry field with the value `text` for the attribute `type`.

accesskey

You can define a shortcut key to access the form element using `accesskey`. Assign the attribute a single letter and it will be executed when you hit this key with the appropriate shortcut key. This key is dependent on the browser and operational system.

autocomplete

Switches the auto completion function on (`on`) or (`off`).

disabled

This sole attribute ensures that the form element is registered as inactive and prevents the element from functioning.

maxlength

Gives the maximum code length for the entry text.

name

Gives the name for the form element to ensure that it can be identified by scripts. The value of the attribute is also given in the evaluation of the form.

readonly

This sole attribute states that the content of this form element may not be altered by the reader.

size

Gives the named code length for the entry text.

tabindex

Gives the tab index of the form element. Positive values stand for the position of the element in the list of objects activated by [⇥] . Negative values mean that the element does not appear in the tab-index.

value

Gives the return value to the script.

vcard_name

Gives the field name of the personal Microsoft visiting card (vcard). The value of the card should be preset. The content of this field is forwarded to the recipient of the form data, when the form has been sent out.

Value	Meaning
vCard.Business.City	Business:city
vCard.Business.Country	Business:country
vCard.Business.Fax	Business:fax
vCard.Business.Phone	Business:phone
vCard.Business.State	Business:state
vCard.Business.StreetAddress	Business:street address
vCard.Business.URL	Business:URL
vCard.Business.ZipCode	Business:zip code
vCard.Cellular	Cellular
vCard.Company	Company
vCard.Department	Department
vCard.DisplayName	Display name
vCard.Email	E-mail
vCard.FirstName	First name
vCard.Gender	Gender
vCard.Home.City	Home:city
vCard.Home.Country	Home:country
vCard.Home.Fax	Home:fax
vCard.Home.Phone	Home:phone
vCard.Home.State	Home:state

Value	Meaning
vCard.Home.StreetAddress	Home:street address
vCard.Home.ZipCode	Home:zip code
vCard.Homepage	Homepage
vCard.JobTitle	Job title
vCard.LastName	Last name
vCard.MiddleName	Middle name
vCard.Notes	Notes
vCard.Office	Office
vCard.Pager	Pager

Table 2.45 *Values for vcard name in <input type ="text">*

See:

`<button>`, `<fieldset>`, `<form>`, `<keygen>`, `<label>`, `<legend>`, `<optgroup>`, `<option>`, `<select>`, `<textarea>`

2.9.6   *<isindex>*

Tag/Attribute	2.0	3.0	3.2	4.0	Internet Explorer	Netscape
`<isindex>`	X	X	X	X	1.0	1.0
action					1.0	1.0
prompt		X	X	X	1.0	1.0

This tag is necessary to activate a specific interactive search in your HTML document.

action

Gives the address of a script which processes the `<isindex>` data.

prompt

Gives an alternative user query which appears when the user wants to activate a search.

Example:

`<isindex prompt ="Your search query:">`

See:

`<base>`, `<link>`, `<meta>`, `<nextid>`, `<scripts>`, `<style>`, `<title>`

2.10 K

2.10.1 <kbd>

Tag/Attribute	2.0	3.0	3.2	4.0	Internet Explorer	Netscape
<kbd>	X	X	X	X	1.0	1.0

This text formats the enclosed text in such a way that it can be recognized as a key entry. Generally it is displayed in a typeface, in which all letters are of the same width.

Example:

```
Enter <kbd>anonymous</kbd>.
```

See:

<abbr>, <b>, <big>, <blink>, <em>, <font>, <i>, <q>, <s>, <samp>, <small>, <strike>, <strong>, <sub>, <sup>, <tt>, <u>, <var>

2.10.2 <keygen>

Tag/Attribute	2.0	3.0	3.2	4.0	Internet Explorer	Netscape
<keygen>						3.0
challenge						3.0
name						3.0

This tag produces a code, which can be applied in the Netscape in forms, to ensure that data transfer is made more secure.

challenge

Is taken as a basis for the code, which was produced accidentally.

name

Gives a name for this form element to ensure that it can be addressed using scripts.

Example:

```
<form method ="post" action="http://www.address.com/secret/
a_script.cgi">
    <keygen name ="Code" challenge ="0815">
    <input type = "text" name = "Entry">
</form>
```

See:

```
<button>, <fieldset>, <form>, <input>, <label>, <legend>,
<optgroup>, <option>, <select>, <textarea>
```

2.11 L

2.11.1 <label>

Tag/Attribute	2.0	3.0	3.2	4.0	Internet Explorer	Netscape
`<label>`				X	4.0B2	
`accesskey`				X	4.0B2	
`for`				X	4.0B2	

This tag is used to add a description to form fields and to simplify navigation within the forms.

accesskey

You can define a shortcut key to access the form element using `accesskey`. Assign the attribute a single letter and it will be executed when you hit this key with the appropriate shortcut key. This key is dependent on the browser and operational system.

for

States to which form field this marking is allocated.

Example:

```
<form>
  <fieldset>
    <legend accesskey ="b" tabindex =1>
      Order newsletter
    </legend>
    <label accesskey ="j">
      <input type="radio" name=news value="yes">yes
    </label><br>
    <label accesskey ="n">
      <input type="radio" name =news value ="no">no
    </label><br>
  </fieldset>
</form>
```

`<button>`, `<fieldset>`, `<form>`, `<input>`, `<keygen>`, `<legend>`, `<optgroup>`, `<option>`, `<select>`, `<textarea>`

2.11.2   *<legend>*

Tag/Attribute	2.0	3.0	3.2	4.0	Internet Explorer	Netscape
`<legend>`				X	4.0B2	
`accesskey`				X	4.0	
`align`				X	4.0B2	

This tag gives the description for a `<fieldset>`.

accesskey

You can define a shortcut key to access the form element using `accesskey`. Assign the attribute a single letter and it will be executed when you hit this key with the appropriate shortcut key. This key is dependent on the browser and operational system.

align

Gives the horizontal alignment within the legend.

Value	Meaning
`center`	The content is aligned to the center.
`left`	The content is aligned to the left.
`right`	The content is aligned to the right.

Table 2.46   *The values for align in <legend>*

Example:

```
<form>
  <fieldset>
    <legend accesskey="b" tabindex=1>
      Order newsletter
    </legend>
    <label accesskey="j">
      <input type="radio" name=news value="yes">yes
    </label><br>
    <label accesskey="n">
      <input type="radio" name=news value="no">no
    </label><br>
  </fieldset>
</form>
```

See:

`<button>`, `<fieldset>`, `<form>`, `<input>`, `<keygen>`, `<label>`, `<optgroup>`, `<option>`, `<select>`, `<textarea>`

2.11.3   <li>

Tag/Attribute	2.0	3.0	3.2	4.0	Internet Explorer	Netscape
`<li>`	X	X	X	X	1.0	1.0
clear		X				
type			X	X	1.0	1.0
value			X	X	1.0	1.0

This tag defines a list element. It is inserted in all current list types.

clear

This attribute was supplemented to ensure that the user can work with images, which are moved to the left or right by the attribute `align` in `<img>`. It can be used when working with all objects, which are moved by `align`.

Value	Meaning
none	A normal word wrap is produced.
left	The line is wrapped and the next line should be inserted in such a way that the left border is free of images (or other objects).
right	The line is wrapped and the next line should be inserted in such a way that the right border is free of images (or other objects).
all	The line is wrapped and the next line should be inserted in such a way that all borders are free of images (or other objects).

Table 2.47 *The values for clear in <li>*

type

States which list points should be used.

Value	Meaning
A	A, B, C, D, ...
a	a, b, c, d, ...
I	I, II, III, IV, ...
i	i, ii, iii, iv, ...
1	1, 2, 3, 4, ...
disc	disc
square	square
circle	circle

Table 2.48 *The values for type in <li>*

value

Gives another value for the enumeration than the current following value according to the last list element.

Example:

```
<dir>
  <li type="disc"> disc
  <li type="circle"> circle
  <li type="square"> square
</dir>
```

See:

```
<dd>, <dir>, <dl>, <dt>, <menu>, <ol>, <ul>
```

2.11.4 <link>

Tag/Attribute	2.0	3.0	3.2	4.0	Internet Explorer	Netscape
<link>	X	X	X	X	3.0B1	4.0B2
charset				X		
disabled					4.0	
href	X	X	X	X	3.0B1	4.0B2
hreflang				X		
rel	X	X	X	X	3.0B1	4.0B2
rev	X	X	X	X	4.0	
src						4.0
target				X		
type				X	3.0B1	4.0B2

This tag is used in the HTML head and gives a link to a document, which is connected to the current document. This connection is set in `rel`.

charset

This attribute contains the target code. The standard value is `ISO-8859-1`.

disabled

This sole attribute states that the link is not currently available.

href

The target address of the link.

hreflang

This attribute states the main language of the target.

rel

States the connection of the link with the document.

rev

This attribute corresponds to the reversal of `rel`. It states the connection between the target and the page.

src

Gives the address of a typeface which can be downloaded.

target

The name of the target frame, in which the target of the link should be displayed, is entered here.

type

States the MIME type of the target.

Example:

```
<link rel="home" href="http://www.my homepage.com">
```

See:

```
<base>, <isindex>, <meta>, <nextid>, <scripts>, <style>,
<title>
```

2.11.5   *<listing>*

Tag/Attribute	2.0	3.0	3.2	4.0	Internet Explorer	Netscape
`<listing>`	X	X	X	X	1.0	1.0

Repeats the source text until the final tag `</listing>` word for word.

Example:

```
<listing>
 Tags can be written out here (e.g. <br>) and they appear on
the screen as they are written without having any effect.
</listing>
```

2.12   M

2.12.1   *<map>*

Tag/Attribute	2.0	3.0	3.2	4.0	Internet Explorer	Netscape
`<map>`			X	X	1.0	2.0
`name`			X	X	1.0	2.0

This tag is necessary for the production of image maps. It contains the hot areas as `<area>` and the image in `<img>` with an assigned `ismap` attribute.

name

A name for the image map (which is also a bookmark) is entered here. This enables the user to jump back to this position in the document.

Example:

```
<map name="An image map">
  <area shape="rectangle" coords="10,20,30,40"
  href="http://www.address.com/a.htm">
  <area shape="circle" COORDS="60,50,20" href="
  http://www.address.com/b.htm ">
  <area shape="polygon" coords="5,100,10,110,0,110" href="
  http://www.address.com/c.htm ">
</map>
```

See:

`<area>`, `<bgsound>`, `<img>`, `<object>`

2.12.2 *<marquee>*

Tag/Attribute	2.0	3.0	3.2	4.0	Internet Explorer	Netscape
`<marquee>`					2.0	
`behavior`					2.0	
`bgcolor`					2.0	
`direction`					2.0	
`height`					2.0	
`hspace`					2.0	
`loop`					2.0	
`scrollamount`					2.0	
`scrolldelay`					2.0	
`truespeed`					4.0BI	
`vspace`					2.0	
`width`					2.0	

This tag produces running script, which can be controlled.

behavior

Defines the behavior of the running script.

Value	Meaning
`scroll`	The text appears on one side and runs to the opposite side, where it disappears again, then the process is repeated.
`slide`	The text appears on one side and runs to the opposite side, where it disappears again, then it stops.
`alternate`	The text swings from one side to the opposite side and back.

Table 2.49 *The values for behavior in <marquee>*

bgcolor

The background color for the running script is set here. RGB values and, for many browsers, predefined color values apply (see Appendix B).

direction

Gives the direction in which the running script should move.

Value	Meaning
left	The text moves to the left.
right	The text moves to the right.
up	The text moves up.
down	The text moves down.

Table 2.50 *The values for direction in <marquee>*

height

Gives the height of the running script field in pixels or percentile to the browser window height.

hspace

Gives the left and right gap between the running script and all other HTML components in pixels.

loop

States how often the running script should repeat the animation process. The value -1 is planned for an endless band.

scrollamount

Gives the horizontal gap between two phases of the running script in pixels.

scrolldelay

Gives the delay between the individual phases of the running script in milliseconds.

truespeed

This sole attribute states that the scrolldelay values should be adhered to exactly. If this attribute is missing, values less than 60 will be rounded up to 60.

vspace

Gives the upper and lower gap of the running script to all other HTML components in pixels.

width

Gives the width of the running script field in pixels or percentile to the browser window width.

Example:

```
<marquee loop ="infinite" behavior ="alternate"
WIDTH=600 HEIGHT =50>
  I am a running script.
</marquee>
```

See:

`<address>`, `<blockquote>`, `<center>`, `<cite>`, `<code>`, `<dfn>`, `<h1>`, `<h2>`, `<h3>`, `<h4>`, `<h5>`, `<h6>`, `<multicol>`, `<p>`, `<pre>`

2.12.3   `<menu>`

Tag/Attribute	2.0	3.0	3.2	4.0	Internet Explorer	Netscape
`<menu>`	X	X	X	X	1.0	1.0
`compact`	X	X	X	X		
`type`						4.0

This tag functions exactly as `<ul>`, but is specifically for one line list elements.

compact

This sole attribute states that at least one presentation should be selected, which saves space.

type

States which list points should be used.

Value	Meaning
A	A, B, C, D, ...
a	a, b, c, d, ...
I	I, II, III, IV, ...
i	i, ii, iii, iv, ...
1	1, 2, 3, 4, ...
disc	disc
square	square
circle	circle

Table 2.51   The values for type in `<menu>`

Example:

```
<menu>
  <li type ="disc">disc
  <li type ="circle">circle
  <li type ="square">square
</menu>
```

See:

`<dd>`, `<dir>`, `<dl>`, `<dt>`, `<li>`, `<ol>`, `<ul>`

2.12.4   *<meta>*

Tag/Attribute	2.0	3.0	3.2	4.0	Internet Explorer	Netscape
`<meta>`	X	X	X	X	2.0	1.1
`content`	X	X	X	X	2.0	1.1
`http-equiv`	X	X	X	X	2.0	1.1
`name`	X	X	X	X	2.0	1.1
`scheme`				X		

This tag represents a universal information mechanism, which provides information on the content of the HTML page. Many search engines produce, for example, lists of key words on the tag `<meta>`.

content

Gives the value, which refers to `name`.

http-equiv

Gives a text, which is sent to the server with the http head before the actual HTML text.

name

Gives a description for the information.

> **Tip** If this attribute is not used, `http-equiv` is necessary.

scheme

Gives additional information on the format of `content`, if several formats should be supported.

Example:

```
<meta http-equiv ="refresh" content ="10; url=http://
www.address.com/next.htm">
```

See:

```
<base>, <isindex>, <link>, <nextid>, <scripts>, <style>,
<title>
```

2.12.5   *<multicol>*

Tag/Attribute	2.0	3.0	3.2	4.0	Internet Explorer	Netscape
`<multicol>`						3.0B5
`cols`						3.0B5
`gutter`						3.0B5
`width`						3.0B5

This tag defines several columns of the same width, in which the text is incorporated fluently.

cols

Gives the number of columns available.

gutter

Gives the gap between the individual columns in pixels.

width

Gives the width of the columns in pixels.

Example:

```
<multicol cols =2 gutter =20>
   The text is distributed evenly between two columns.
   Images and other HTML elements are distributed.

</multicol>
```

See:

```
<address>, <blockquote>, <center>, <cite>, <code>, <dfn>,
<h1>, <h2>, <h3>, <h4>, <h5>, <h6>, <marquee>, <p>, <pre>
```

2.13 N

2.13.1   *<nextid>*

Tag/Attribute	2.0	3.0	3.2	4.0	Internet Explorer	Netscape
<nextid>	X	X				
n	X	X				

This tag was previously used for the naming of <a> tags.

Tip Please do not use this tag anymore!

See:

<base>, <isindex>, <link>, <meta>, <scripts>, <style>, <title>

2.13.2   *<nobr>*

Tag/Attribute	2.0	3.0	3.2	4.0	Internet Explorer	Netscape
<nobr>					1.0	1.0

Marks a text passage which should not contain an automatically generated word wrap.

Example:

```
<nobr>
  This complete text should be in one row. This
  sentence should be in the first row. Only at this point
  <br>is the text manually wrapped.
</nobr>
```

See:

, <wbr>

2.13.3   *<noembed>*

Tag/Attribute	2.0	3.0	3.2	4.0	Internet Explorer	Netscape
<noembed>					3.0B2	2.0

This tag is used within <embed> ... </embed>. It marks a source code, which should only be carried out if the browser can not process the tag <embed>.

Example:

```
<embed src ="a_song.mid" controls>
  <noembed>
    Your browser does not support the inclusion of
    <a HREF ="a_song.mid">song</a>.
  </noembed>
</embed>
```

See:

<applet>, <embed>, <iframe>, <noscript>, <param>, <script>

2.13.4   *<noframes>*

Tag/Attribute	2.0	3.0	3.2	4.0	Internet Explorer	Netscape
<noframes>				X	3.0A1	2.0

This tag marks the source code, which should only be carried out if the browser cannot process the tag <frameset>.

Example:

```
<html>
  <head>
    <title>A frame example</title>
  </head>
  <frameset rows=20%,60%,20%>
    <frame src="a.htm" name ="above">
    <frameset cols=50%,50%>
      <frame src="b.htm" name ="center left">
      <frame src="c.htm" name ="center right">
    </frameset>
    <frame src="d.htm" name ="lower">
  </frameset>
  <noframes>
    <head>
      <title> A frame example (Your browser is too old)
      </title>
    </head>
    <body>
      <center>
        WARNING!<P>
        YOU ARE USING A BROWSER, WHICH DOES NOT SUPPORT
```

```
FRAMES: PLEASE CLICK
       <a href="a.htm"> HERE </a>,
TO OBTAIN A VERSION WITH NO FRAMES<p>
      </center>
    </body>
  </noframes>
</html>
```

See:

`<frame>`, `<frameset>`

2.13.5   *<noscript>*

Tag/Attribute	2.0	3.0	3.2	4.0	Internet Explorer	Netscape
`<noscript>`			X	3.0	3.0B5

This tag marks the source code, which should only be carried out if the browser can not process the tag `<noscript>`.

Example:

```
<script language ="JavaScript">
  <!-- document. Write("This is a JavaScript.") -->
</script>
<noscript>
  This is not a JavaScript.
</noscript>
```

See:

`<applet>`, `<embed>`, `<iframe>`, `<noembed>`, `<param>`, `<script>`

2.14   O

2.14.1   *<object>*

Tag/Attribute	2.0	3.0	3.2	4.0	Internet Explorer	Netscape
`<object>`				X	3.0AI	
`accesskey`					4.0	
`align`				X	3.0AI	
`border`				X		
`classid`				X	3.0AI	

Tag/Attribute	2.0	3.0	3.2	4.0	Internet Explorer	Netscape
code					4.0	
codebase				X	3.0A1	
codetype				X	3.0A1	
data				X	3.0A1	
declare				X		
height				X	3.0A1	
hspace				X		
name				X	3.0A1	
standby				X		
tabindex				X		
type				X	3.0A1	
usemap				X		
vspace				X		
width				X	3.0A1	

This tag is a universal multimedia insertion tag.

accesskey

You can define a shortcut key to access the object using `accesskey`. Assign the attribute a single letter and it will be executed when you hit this key with the appropriate shortcut key. This key is dependent on the browser and operational system.

align

Gives the horizontal alignment of the object.

Value	Meaning
center	The object is aligned centrally.
left	The object is aligned to the left.
right	The object is aligned to the right.

Table 2.52 *The values for align in <object>*

border

Gives the width of the frame, which is shown around an image, when it is used as an anchor for a link. It contains the color which a normal text link would have.

classid

Gives the address to the source code of the object.

code

Refers to the class of the object. The URL is relative to codebase or stated absolutely.

codebase

Gives the register in which the code can be found and to which code should refer.

codetype

Gives the MIME format of the code.

data

Gives an address to the object data (e.g. for an image).

declare

This sole attribute states that the object must firstly be loaded if it has been called up by an HTML element or by a script.

height

Gives the height of the object in pixels.

hspace

Gives the left and right gap from the object to all other HTML components in pixels.

name

Gives the name of the object, when it reacts as a form element, to ensure that it can be identified by the scripts. The value of the attribute is also stated in the evaluation of the form.

standby

Gives a text which is shown as long as the object is loaded by the browser.

tabindex

Gives the tab index of the object. Positive values stand for the position of the object in the list of objects activated by 🔛. Negative values mean that the object does not appear in the tab index.

type

Gives the MIME type of the object.

usemap

Gives the address of the image map specifications from the client side.

vspace

Gives the upper and lower gap of the object to all other HTML components in pixels.

width

Gives the width of the object in pixels.

See:

`<area>, <bgsound>, <img>, <map>`

2.14.2   <ol>

Tag/Attribute	2.0	3.0	3.2	4.0	Internet Explorer	Netscape
`<ol>`	X	X	X	X	1.0	1.0
`clear`		X				
`compact`	X	X	X	X		
`start`			X	X	1.0	1.0
`type`			X	X	1.0	1.0

This tag produces an ordered (enumerated) list.

clear

This attribute was supplemented to be able to work with images, which are moved left or right by the attribute `align` in `<img>`. It can be used when working with all objects, which are moved by `align`.

Value	Meaning
`none`	A normal word wrap is produced.
`left`	The line is wrapped and the next line should be inserted in such a way that the left border is free of images (or other objects).
`right`	The line is wrapped and the next line should be inserted in such a way that the right border is free of images (or other objects).
`all`	The line is wrapped and the next line should be inserted in such a way that all borders are free of images (or other objects).

Table 2.53 *The values for clear in <ol>*

compact

This sole attribute states that at least one presentation should be selected which saves space.

start

Gives the start value of the enumeration.

type

States which list points should be used.

Value	Meaning
A	A, B, C, D, ...
a	a, b, c, d, ...
I	I, II, III, IV, ...
i	i, ii, iii, iv, ...
1	1, 2, 3, 4, ...
disc	disc
square	square
circle	circle

Table 2.54 *The values for type in <ol>*

Example:

```
<ol>
  <li type="disc">disc
  <li type="circle">circle
  <li type="square">square
</ol>
```

See:

<dd>, <dir>, <dl>, <dt>, <li>, <menu>, <ul>

2.14.3 <optgroup>

Tag/Attribute	2.0	3.0	3.2	4.0	Internet Explorer	Netscape
<optgroup>				X		
disable				X		
label				X		

This tag summarizes several <option> tags from a selected field and arranges them in order of importance.

disable

This sole attribute states that this element was temporarily deactivated.

label

Gives an abbreviation for the option group.

Example:

```
<form>
  <select name="Products">
    <option value="Mon">Monitor
    <option value="Pri">Printer
    <optgroup label="Computer">
      <option value="HDD">Hard disc
      <option value="Cas">Casing
      <option value="CPU">Processor
    </optgroup>
  </select>
</form>
```

See:

`<button>`, `<fieldset>`, `<form>`, `<input>`, `<keygen>`, `<label>`,
`<legend>`, `<option>`, `<select>`, `<textarea>`

2.14.4   *<option>*

Tag/Attribute	2.0	3.0	3.2	4.0	Internet Explorer	Netscape
`<option>`	X	X	X	X	1.0	1.0
`disable`		X		X		
`label`				X		
`selected`	X	X	X	X	1.0	1.0
`value`	X	X	X	X	1.0	1.0

Gives the individual options for a selection field.

disable

This sole attribute states that this element was temporarily deactivated.

label

Gives an abbreviation for the option.

selected

This sole attribute states that this option should be selected in the presetting.

value

Gives the value for this element, which should be sent to the form, if this element is selected.

Example:

```
<form>
  <select name="Products">
    <option value="Mon">Monitor
    <option value="Pri">Printer
    <optgroup label="Computer">
      <option value="HDD">Hard disc
      <option value="Cas">Casing
      <option value="CPU">Processor
    </optgroup>
  </select>
</form>
```

See:

`<button>`, `<fieldset>`, `<form>`, `<input>`, `<keygen>`, `<label>`, `<legend>`, `<optgroup>`, `<select>`, `<textarea>`

2.15 P

2.15.1   *<p>*

Tag/Attribute	2.0	3.0	3.2	4.0	Internet Explorer	Netscape
`<p>`	X	X	X	X	1.0	1.0
`align`		X	X	X	1.0	1.0
`clear`		X				

Produces a paragraph.

align

Gives the horizontal alignment within the paragraph.

Value	Meaning
`center`	The content is aligned centrally.
`left`	The content is aligned to the left.
`right`	The content is aligned to the right.

Table 2.55 *The values for align in <p>*

clear

This attribute was supplemented to be able to work with images that are moved left or right by the attribute `align` in `<img>`. It can be used when working with all objects, which are moved by `align`.

Value	Meaning
none	A normal word wrap is produced.
left	The line is wrapped and the next line should be inserted in such a way that the left border is free of images (or other objects).
right	The line is wrapped and the next line should be inserted in such a way that the right border is free of images (or other objects).
all	The line is wrapped and the next line should be inserted in such a way that all borders are free of images (or other objects).

Table 2.56 *The values for clear in `<p>`*

Example:

```
This is a demo text.
<p>This is a self-contained paragraph.</p>
And the text continues here.
```

See:

`<address>`, `<blockquote>`, `<center>`, `<cite>`, `<code>`, `<dfn>`, `<h1>`, `<h2>`, `<h3>`, `<h4>`, `<h5>`, `<h6>`, `<marquee>`, `<multicol>`, `<pre>`

2.15.2   `<param>`

Tag/Attribute	2.0	3.0	3.2	4.0	Internet Explorer	Netscape
`<param>`			X	X	3.0AI	2.0
name			X	X	3.0AI	2.0
type				X		
value			X	X	3.0AI	2.0
valuetype				X		

This tag is responsible for the parameter submission to embedded objects (`<object>`, `<applet>`, etc).

name

This attribute gives the name of the parameter.

type

Gives the MIME types of the data source defined in `value`, when `valuetype` has the value `"ref"`.

value

Gives the value of the parameter `name`.

valuetype

Gives the type of value `value`.

Value	Meaning
data	The value is forwarded directly to the object.
ref	The `value` is identified here as URL.
object	Identifies `value` as an object internal reference.

Table 2.57 *The values for value type in <param>*

Example:

```
<applet codebase="http://www.address.com/java/"
code="an_applet.class" >
  <param name="Line1" value="Textline 1">
  <param name="Line2" value="Textline 2">
  <param name="Line2" value="Textline 2">
  Your browser is not Java compatible!<br>
</applet>
```

See:

`<applet>, <embed>, <iframe>, <noembed>, <noscript>, <script>`

2.15.3   *<plaintext>*

Tag/Attribute	2.0	3.0	3.2	4.0	Internet Explorer	Netscape
`<plaintext>`	X	X	X	X	1.0	1.0

The following text is reproduced word for word on the screen. Even a closing `</plaintext>` tag is ignored.

Example:

```
Normal HTML text is displayed here.
<plaintext>
And from this point everything is reproduced 1:1 on the
screen.
```

2.15.4   <pre>

Tag/Attribute	2.0	3.0	3.2	4.0	Internet Explorer	Netscape
<pre>	X	X	X	X	1.0	1.0
width	X	X	X	X		

This tag marks preformatted text. All spaces, tabs and line wraps are written on the screen.

width

Gives the text width in points.

Example:

```
<pre width=40>
    This text is specially aligned to
display 40 characters.  As can be seen
there are no problems here.
</pre>
```

Result:

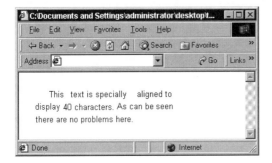

Figure 2.3 *Preformatted text with 40 point width*

See:

```
<address>, <blockquote>, <center>, <cite>, <code>, <dfn>,
<h1>, <h2>, <h3>, <h4>, <h5>, <h6>, <marquee>, <multicol>,
<p>
```

2.16 Q

2.16.1 <q>

Tag/Attribute	2.0	3.0	3.2	4.0	Internet Explorer	Netscape
`<q>`				X	4.0	
`cite`				X		

This tag identifies short quotes. The inverted commas are positioned by the browser.

cite

Gives a URL, which identifies the source of the quote.

Example:

```
<q cite="http://www.spectrosoftware.com">...and life
becomes colorful</q>.
```

See:

```
<abbr>, <b>, <big>, <blink>, <em>, <font>, <i>, <kbd>, <s>,
<samp>, <small>, <strike>, <strong>, <sub>, <sup>, <tt>,
<u>, <var>
```

2.17 R

2.17.1 <rt>

Tag/Attribute	2.0	3.0	3.2	4.0	Internet Explorer	Netscape
`<rt>`					5.0B2	
`name`					5.0B2	

This tag is used within `<ruby> ... </ruby>`. It produces the help text for its content.

name

Gives the name of the help text, to define it as the target point for hyperlinks.

Example:

```
Virtual worlds are defined in
<ruby>VRML<rt>pronounced: vermel</rt></ruby>
```

Result:

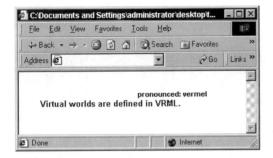

Figure 2.4   *A description of the word "VRML" is given here*

See:

```
<ruby>
```

2.17.2   *<ruby>*

Tag/Attribute	2.0	3.0	3.2	4.0	Internet Explorer	Netscape
`<ruby>`					5.0B2	
`name`					5.0B2	

Marks a short text passage, to provide a brief explanation using `<rt>`. This appears in small typeface over the content of `<ruby>` ... `</ruby>`. This mechanism was specifically introduced for far eastern languages, to provide assistance with pronunciation. It can also be used for other purposes, as the user deems reasonable.

name

Gives the name of the help text, to define it as target point for hyperlinks.

Example:

```
Virtual worlds are defined in
<ruby>VRML<rt>some say "vermel"</rt></ruby>
```

See:

```
<rt>
```

2.18   S

2.18.1   \<s>

Tag/Attribute	2.0	3.0	3.2	4.0	Internet Explorer	Netscape
\<s>		X		X	1.0	3.0B5

Displays the crossed out enclosed text.

Example:

```
<s>This text is crossed out,</s> but this is not.
```

See:

\<abbr>, \<b>, \<big>, \<blink>, \<em>, \<font>, \<i>, \<kbd>, \<q>, \<samp>, \<small>, \<strike>, \<strong>, \<sub>, \<sup>, \<tt>, \<u>, \<var>

2.18.2   \<samp>

Tag/Attribute	2.0	3.0	3.2	4.0	Internet Explorer	Netscape
\<samp>	X	X	X	X	1.0	1.0

Formats a text as example. Generally presented in the typeface "courier".

Example:

```
Enter the following text:<br>
<samp>This is a test.</samp>
```

See:

\<abbr>, \<b>, \<big>, \<blink>, \<em>, \<font>, \<i>, \<kbd>, \<q>, \<s>, \<small>, \<strike>, \<strong>, \<sub>, \<sup>, \<tt>, \<u>, \<var>

2.18.3   \<script>

Tag/Attribute	2.0	3.0	3.2	4.0	Internet Explorer	Netscape
\<script>				X	3.0B1	2.0B3
charset				X		
defer				X	4.0	
event				X	4.0	
for				X	4.0	
language				X	3.0B1	2.0B3

TAKE THHAT!

Tag/Attribute	2.0	3.0	3.2	4.0	Internet Explorer	Netscape
src				X	3.02	3.0B5
type				X	4.0	

The tag `<script>` denotes script languages. JavaScript is an example of such a script language. `<script>` is therefore used, to differentiate JavaScript text from HTML source code.

charset

This attribute states which code should be used for the script. The standard setting is ISO-8859-1.

defer

This sole attribute does not require value allocation. If it is used, the browser is informed that the script does not produce any screen distribution.

event

Gives the result for which the script was written. We will tell you more about this later.

for

States which element is linked to this script. Again, we will tell you more about this later.

language

This attribute states which language was used for the script.

src

An external data source can be addressed here. This makes sense, for example, when a number of HTML files use the same script.

type

This attribute gives the MIME type of the script source code.

Example:

```
<script language="JavaScript">
  <!-- document.write("This is a JavaScript.") -->
</script>
<noscript>
  This is not a JavaScript.
</noscript>
```

See:

<base>, <isindex>, <link>, <meta>, <nextid>, <style>,
<title>, <applet>, <embed>, <iframe>, <noembed>,
<noscript>, <param>

2.18.4 <select>

Tag/Attribute	2.0	3.0	3.2	4.0	Internet Explorer	Netscape
<select>	X	X	X	X	1.0	1.0
accesskey					4.0B1	
align					4.0	
disabled		X		X	4.0B1	
multiple	X	X	X	X	1.0	1.0
name	X	X	X	X	1.0	1.0
size	X		X	X	1.0	1.0
tabindex				X	4.0B1	

Gives a selection list, in which the elements have been set by <option>.

accesskey

You can define a shortcut key to access the selection field using accesskey. Assign the attribute a single letter and it will be executed when you hit this key with the appropriate shortcut key. This key is dependent on the browser and system.

align

Gives the horizontal alignment of the selection field.

Value	Meaning
center	The field is aligned centrally.
left	The field is aligned to the left.
right	The field is aligned to the right.

Table 2.58 *The values for align in <select>*

disabled

States that the selection list is temporarily deactivated.

multiple

States that several options can be selected.

name

Gives the name of the form element to ensure that it can be identified by scripts. The value of the attribute is also stated in the form evaluation.

size

Gives the shown point length of the options.

tabindex

Gives the tab index for the selection field. Positive values stand for the position of the field in the list of objects activated by ⭾. Negative values mean that the selection field does not appear in the tab index.

Example:

```
<form>
  <select name="Products">
    <option value="Mon">Monitor
    <option value="Pri">Printer
    <optgroup label="Computer">
      <option value="HDD">Hard disc
      <option value="Cas">Casing
      <option value="CPU">Processor
    </optgroup>
  </select>
</form>
```

See:

`<button>`, `<fieldset>`, `<form>`, `<input>`, `<keygen>`, `<label>`, `<legend>`, `<optgroup>`, `<option>`, `<textarea>`

2.18.5   *<small>*

Tag/Attribute	2.0	3.0	3.2	4.0	Internet Explorer	Netscape
`<small>`		X	X	X	3.0AI	1.1

States that the enclosed text should be displayed in a smaller typeface.

Example:

```
<small>This text is printed in small typeface,</small> but
this is not.
```

See:

`<abbr>`, `<b>`, `<big>`, `<blink>`, `<em>`, `<font>`, `<i>`, `<kbd>`, `<q>`, `<s>`, `<samp>`, `<strike>`, `<strong>`, `<sub>`, `<sup>`, `<tt>`, `<u>`, `<var>`

2.18.6   <spacer>

Tag/Attribute	2.0	3.0	3.2	4.0	Internet Explorer	Netscape
<spacer>						3.0B5
align						3.0B5
height						3.0B5
size						3.0B5
type						3.0B5
width						3.0B5

This tag produces a free variable parameter, used to position more generous gaps in HTML documents.

align

Gives the alignment of the text, which also applies to the variable parameter.

Value	Meaning
middle	The text is aligned vertically in the center.
left	The text is aligned to the left.
right	The text is aligned to the right.
top	The text is aligned to the top.
bottom	The text is aligned to the bottom.

Table 2.59   *The values for align in <spacer>*

height

Gives the height of the variable parameter in pixels.

size

This attribute gives the height or the width in pixels according to the value of type.

type

Gives the type of space maker.

Value	Meaning
horizontal	Refers to a height space.
vertical	Refers to a width space.
block	Refers to a height and width space.

Table 2.60   *The values for type in <spacer>*

width

Gives the width of the variable parameter in pixels.

2.18.7   *<span>*

Tag/Attribute	2.0	3.0	3.2	4.0	Internet Explorer	Netscape
`<span>`				X	3.0B1	4.0B2

This tag is used to carry out style sheet formatting directly in the HTML source text. This would be implemented when a format can be allocated via CSS, which would not be possible via HTML.

2.18.8   *<strike>*

Tag/Attribute	2.0	3.0	3.2	4.0	Internet Explorer	Netscape
`<strike>`			X	X	1.0	1.1

Displays the enclosed text crossed out.

Example:

```
<strike>This text is crossed out,</strike> this text is
not.
```

See:

```
<abbr>, <b>, <big>, <blink>, <em>, <font>, <i>, <kbd>, <q>,
<s>, <samp>, <small>, <strong>, <sub>, <sup>, <tt>, <u>,
<var>
```

2.18.9   *<strong>*

Tag/Attribute	2.0	3.0	3.2	4.0	Internet Explorer	Netscape
`<strong>`	X	X	X	X	1.0	1.0

Highlights the enclosed text (generally in bold).

Example:

```
<strong>This text is highlighted,</strong> but this is not.
```

See:

```
<abbr>, <b>, <big>, <blink>, <em>, <font>, <i>, <kbd>, <q>,
<s>, <samp>, <small>, <strike>, <sub>, <sup>, <tt>, <u>,
<var>
```

2.18.10 `<style>`

Tag/Attribute	2.0	3.0	3.2	4.0	Internet Explorer	Net-scape
`<style>`		X	X	X	3.0B1	4.0B2
`disabled`					4.0	
`media`				X	4.0	
`title`				X		
`type`				X	3.0B1	4.0B2

This tag is called up in the head of a HTML page and offers one of several variations for inserting style sheets in the HTML pages.

disabled

This sole attribute states that the inclusion of the style sheets should be ignored for the moment.

media

States for which type of edition the allocation of the style sheets should be used. Several names are possible, when separated by commas.

Value	Meaning
`screen`	The style sheet is used on a computer screen in the issue of a HTML page.
`print`	The style sheet is used on a printer in the issue of a HTML page.
`projection`	The style sheet is used on a projection machine in the issue of a HTML page.
`braille`	The style sheet is used on a braille machine in the issue of a HTML page.
`speech`	The style sheet is used via language in the issue of a HTML page.
`all`	The style sheet is used on all of the above in the issue of a HTML page.

Table 2.61 *The values for media in `<style>`*

title

This attribute gives a name to the style sheet, which enables it to address the CSS directly to switch it on or off or to redirect it.

type

Gives the MIME type of the style sheet.

See:

`<base>`, `<isindex>`, `<link>`, `<meta>`, `<nextid>`, `<scripts>`, `<title>`

2.18.11 <sub>

Tag/Attribute	2.0	3.0	3.2	4.0	Internet Explorer	Netscape
<sub>		X	X	X	3.0B1	1.1

States that the enclosed text should be set deeper.

Example:

_{This text is set deeper,} but this is not.

See:

<abbr>, <b>, <big>, <blink>, <em>, <font>, <i>, <kbd>, <q>, <s>, <samp>, <small>, <strike>, <strong>, <sup>, <tt>, <u>, <var>

2.18.12 <sup>

Tag/Attribute	2.0	3.0	3.2	4.0	Internet Explorer	Netscape
<sup>		X	X	X	3.0B1	1.1

Reproduces the enclosed text in its original form.

Example:

^{This text is set higher again,} but this is not.

See:

<abbr>, <b>, <big>, <blink>, <em>, <font>, <i>, <kbd>, <q>, <s>, <samp>, <small>, <strike>, <strong>, <sub>, <tt>, <u>, <var>

2.19 T

2.19.1 <table>

Tag/Attribute	2.0	3.0	3.2	4.0	Internet Explorer	Netscape
<table>		X	X	X	2.0	1.1
align		X	X	X	2.0	2.0
background					2.0	4.0B3
bgcolor				X	2.0	3.0B1
border		X	X	X	2.0	1.1
bordercolor					2.0	4.0
borderdark					2.0	

TAKE THHAT!

Tag/Attribute	2.0	3.0	3.2	4.0	Internet Explorer	Netscape
borderlight					2.0	
cellpadding			X	X	2.0	1.1
cellspacing			X	X	2.0	1.1
cols					3.0A1	4.0B2
datapagesize				X	4.0	
frame				X	3.0A1	
height					2.0	1.1
rules				X	3.0A1	
summary				X		
width		X	X	X	2.0	1.1

This tag defines a table.

align

Gives the horizontal alignment of the table within the browser window.

Value	Meaning
center	The table is aligned centrally.
left	The table is aligned to the left.
right	The table is aligned to the right.

Table 2.62 *The values for align in <table>*

background

Gives the address of a background image for the table.

bgcolor

The background color for the table is set here. RGB values and, for many browsers, predefined color values apply (see Appendix B).

border

Gives the width of the table frame.

border color

The main color for the table frame is set here. RGB values and, for many browsers, predefined color values apply (see Appendix B).

border color dark

The dark color for the table frame is set here in 3D. RGB values and, for many browsers, predefined color values apply (see Appendix B).

border color light

The light color for the table frame is set here in 3D. RGB values and, for many browsers, predefined color values apply (see Appendix B).

cell padding

Gives the gap between the cell content and the cell frame.

cell spacing

Gives the gap between the cells.

cols

Gives the number of columns in the table.

data page size

Gives the size of a data page in endless tables.

frame

States where the outer frame of the table should be drawn.

Value	Meaning
void	The frame is not displayed.
above	A frame only appears on the upper border.
below	A frame only appears on the lower border.
hsides	A frame only appears on the upper and lower border.
vsides	A frame only appears on the left and right border.
lhs	A frame only appears on the left border.
rhs	A frame only appears on the right border.
box	A frame appears on all four sides.
border	A frame appears on all four sides.

Table 2.63 *The values for frame in <table>*

height

Gives the height of the table in pixels or as a percentile of the height of the browser window.

rules

Defines the inner rows in the table.

Value	Meaning
none	The rows are not shown.
groups	Rows, which separate the groups formed by `<thead>`, `<tbody>`, `<tfoot>` and `<colgroup>` are shown.
rows	Horizontal rows are shown.
cols	Vertical rows are shown.
all	All rows between the cells are shown.

Table 2.64 *The values for rules in <table>*

summary

Forwards a summary of the table content. (Important for browsers with language edition).

width

Gives the width of the table in pixels or as a percentile of the width of the browser window.

Example:

```
<table border=1>
  <caption>Browser statistic</caption>
  <tr><th>Browser</th><th>Market share</th></tr>
  <tr><td>Microsoft Internet Explorer</td><td>60.4 %</td>
  </tr>
  <tr><td>Netscape Communicator</td><td>38.5 %</td></tr>
  <tr><td>Others</td><td>1.1 %</td></tr>
</table>
```

See:

`<caption>`, `<col>`, `<colgroup>`, `<thead>`, `<tbody>`, `<tfoot>`, `<th>`, `<td>`, `<tr>`

2.19.2   <tbody>

Tag/Attribute	2.0	3.0	3.2	4.0	Internet Explorer	Netscape
`<tbody>`				X	3.0AI	
align				X	4.0BI	
bgcolor					4.0BI	
char				X		
charoff				X		
valign				X	4.0BI	

Defines the table body in a table.

align

Gives the horizontal alignment within the cells.

Value	Meaning
center	The content is aligned to the center.
left	The content is aligned to the left.
right	The content is aligned to the right.

Table 2.65 *The values for align in <tbody>*

bgcolor

The background color of the cells is set here. RGB values and, for many browsers, predefined color values (see Appendix B) are the standard.

char

The code for aligning the cell content can be given here. The first appearance of this code is relevant.

charoff

Gives the gap to the defined alignment code, which has appeared for the first time in char in pixels.

valign

Gives the vertical alignment within the cells.

Value	Meaning
bottom	The content is aligned to the bottom.
top	The content is aligned to the top.

Table 2.66 *The values for valign in <tbody>*

Example:

```
<table border=1>
  <thead>
    <tr><th colspan=2>Browser statistic</th></td>
  </thead>
  <tbody>
    <tr><th>Browser</th><th>Market share</th></tr>
    <tr><td>Microsoft Internet Explorer</td>
        <td>60.4 %</td>
    </tr>
    <tr><td>Netscape Communicator</td><td>38.5 %</td></tr>
```

```
  <tr><td>Others</td><td>1.1 %</td></tr>
 </tbody>
 <tfoot>
   <tr><td colspan=2>Status: Middle 2000</td></td>
 </tfoot>
</table>
```

See:

```
<caption>, <col>, <colgroup>, <table>, <tfoot>, <th>,
<thead>, <td>, <tr>
```

2.19.3   <td>

Tag/Attribute	2.0	3.0	3.2	4.0	Internet Explorer	Netscape
`<td>`		X	X	X	2.0	1.1
`align`		X	X	X	2.0	1.1
`background`					3.0A1	4.0B3
`bgcolor`				X	2.0	3.0B1
`bordercolor`					2.0	
`bordercolordark`					2.0	
`bordercolorlight`					2.0	
`char`				X		
`charoff`				X		
`colspan`		X	X	X	2.0	1.1
`headers`				X		
`height`			X	X	2.0	1.1
`no wrap`		X	X	X	2.0	1.1
`rowspan`		X	X	X	2.0	1.1
`scope`				X		
`valign`		X	X	X	2.0	1.1
`width`			X	X	2.0	1.1

Defines a data cell in a table.

align

Gives the horizontal alignment within the cells.

Value	Meaning
center	The content is centered.
left	The content is aligned to the left.
right	The content is aligned to the right.

Table 2.67 *The values for align in <td>*

background

Gives the address of a background image for the cells.

bgcolor

The background color of the cells is set here. RGB values and, for many browsers, predefined color values (see Appendix B) are the standard.

bordercolor

The main color for the cell frame is set here. RGB values and, for many browsers, predefined color values apply (see Appendix B).

border color dark

The dark color for the cell frame is set here in 3D. RGB values and, for many browsers, predefined color values apply (see Appendix B).

border color light

The light color for the cell frame is set here in 3D. RGB values and, for many browsers, predefined color values apply (see Appendix B).

char

The code for aligning the cell content can be given here. The first appearance of this code is relevant.

charoff

Gives the gap to the defined alignment code, which has appeared for the first time in char in pixels.

colspan

Gives the number of columns over which the cells extend.

headers

States again to which cell headings the cells belong. This can be an advantage in the language edition. The list elements are separated by spaces.

height

Gives the height of the cells in pixels or as a percentile of the height of the browser window.

TAKE THHAT!

2

no wrap

Gives information as to whether the normal HTML word wrap rules are valid or should be ignored.

Value	Meaning
false	The normal rules apply: text, which has come to the end of the row will be automatically wrapped.
true	Text, which has come to the end of the row, will not be wrapped. Exceptions will only be made in the case of specified formatting (` `, `<p>`, etc).

Table 2.68 *The values for no wrap in `<td>`*

rowspan

Gives the number of rows over which the cells extend.

valign

Gives the vertical alignment within the cells.

Value	Meaning
bottom	The content is aligned to the bottom.
top	The content is aligned to the top.

Table 2.69 *The values for valign in `<td>` and `<th>`*

width

Gives the width of the cells in pixels or as a percentile of the width of the browser window.

Example:

```
<table border=1>
  <caption>Browser statistic</caption>
  <tr><th>Browser</th><th>Market share</th></tr>
  <tr><td>Microsoft Internet Explorer</td><td>60.4 %</td>
  </tr>
  <tr><td>Netscape Communicator</td><td>38.5 %</td></tr>
  <tr><td>Others</td><td>1.1 %</td></tr>
</table>
```

See:

```
<caption>, <col>, <colgroup>, <thead>, <tbody>, <tfoot>,
<table>,  <th>, <tr>
```

2.19.4 <textarea>

Tag/Attribute	2.0	3.0	3.2	4.0	Internet Explorer	Netscape
<textarea>	X	X	X	X	1.0	1.0
accesskey				X	4.0B1	
cols	X	X	X	X	1.0	1.0
disabled		X		X	4.0B1	
name	X	X	X	X	1.0	1.0
readonly				X	4.0B1	
rows	X	X	X	X	1.0	1.0
tabindex				X	4.0B1	
wrap				X	4.0	2.0

Defines a text field in a form.

accesskey

You can define a shortcut key to access the text field using `accesskey`. Assign the attribute a single letter and it will be executed when you hit this key with the appropriate shortcut key. This key is dependent on the browser and operational system.

cols

Gives the text columns of the text field.

disabled

This sole attribute states that this form element was temporarily deactivated.

name

Gives the name of the form element to ensure that it can be identified by scripts. The value of the attribute is also stated in the form evaluation.

readonly

This sole attribute states that the content of this form element may not be changed by the reader.

rows

Gives the text rows of the text field.

tabindex

Gives the tab index of the text field. Positive values stand for the position of the field in the list of objects activated by ⭾. Negative values mean that the text field does not appear in the tab index.

wrap

States how the rows should be wrapped.

Value	Meaning
off	The rows are wrapped in the same way they are typed. If (↵) is not entered, the text will not be wrapped.
soft	The rows are wrapped in the report, but sent in the same way as they were entered.
hard	The rows are wrapped in the report, and sent this way to the script.

Table 2.70 *The values for wrap in <textarea>*

See:

`<button>`, `<fieldset>`, `<form>`, `<input>`, `<keygen>`, `<label>`, `<legend>`, `<optgroup>`, `<option>`, `<select>`

2.19.5   <tfoot>

Tag/Attribute	2.0	3.0	3.2	4.0	Internet Explorer	Netscape
`<tfoot>`				X	3.0AI	
align				X	4.0BI	
bgcolor					4.0BI	
char				X		
charoff				X		
valign				X	4.0BI	

Table 2.71 *Defines the table foot of a table*

align

Gives the horizontal alignment within the cells.

Value	Meaning
center	The content is centered.
left	The content is aligned to the left.
right	The content is aligned to the right.

Table 2.72 *The values for align in <tfoot>*

bgcolor

The background color of the cells is set here. RGB values and, for many browsers, predefined color values (see Appendix B) are the standard.

char

The code for aligning the cell content can be given here. The first appearance of this code is relevant.

charoff

Gives the gap to the defined alignment code, which has appeared for the first time in char in pixels.

valign

Gives the vertical alignment within the cells.

Value	Meaning
bottom	The content is aligned to the bottom.
top	The content is aligned to the top.

Table 2.73 *The values for valign in <tfoot>*

Example:

```
<table border=1>
  <thead>
    <tr><th colspan=2>Browser statistic</th></td>
  </thead>
  <tbody>
    <tr><th>Browser</th><th>Market share</th></tr>
    <tr><td>Microsoft Internet Explorer</td>
        <td>60.4 %</td>
    </tr>
    <tr><td>Netscape Communicator</td><td>38.5 %</td></tr>
    <tr><td>Others</td><td>1.1 %</td></tr>
  </tbody>
  <tfoot>
    <tr><td colspan=2>Status: Middle 2000</td></td>
  </tfoot>
</table>
```

See:

<caption>, <col>, <colgroup>, <table>, <tbody>, <th>, <thead>, <td>, <tr>

2.19.6 <th>

Tag/Attribute	2.0	3.0	3.2	4.0	Internet Explorer	Netscape
`<th>`		X	X	X	2.0	1.1
`abbr`				X		
`align`		X	X	X	2.0	1.1
`axis`		X		X		
`background`					3.0A1	4.0B3
`bgcolor`				X	2.0	3.0B1
`bordercolor`					2.0	
`bordercolor-dark`					2.0	
`bordercolor-light`					2.0	
`char`				X		
`charoff`				X		
`colspan`		X	X	X	2.0	1.1
`height`			X	X	2.0	1.1
`no wrap`		X	X	X	2.0	1.1
`rowspan`		X	X	X	2.0	1.1
`scope`				X		
`valign`		X	X	X	2.0	1.1
`width`			X	X	2.0	1.1

Defines a heading cell in a table.

abbr

Defines an abbreviation for a `<th>` cell.

align

Gives the horizontal alignment within the cells.

Value	Meaning
`center`	The content is centered.
`left`	The content is aligned to the left.
`right`	The content is aligned to the right.

Table 2.74 *The values for align in <th>*

axis

Defines an abbreviation for a `<th>` cell.

background

Gives the address of a background image for the cells.

bgcolor

The background color of the cells is set here. RGB values and, for many browsers, predefined color values (see Appendix B) are the standard.

bordercolor

The main color of the cell frame is set here. RGB values and, for many browsers, predefined color values (see Appendix B) are the standard.

bordercolordark

The dark color for the cell frame is set here in 3D. RGB values and, for many browsers, predefined color values apply (see Appendix B).

bordercolorlight

The light color for the cell frame is set here in 3D. RGB values and, for many browsers, predefined color values apply (see Appendix B).

char

The code for aligning the cell content can be given here. The first appearance of this code is relevant.

charoff

Gives the gap to the defined alignment code, which has appeared for the first time in `char` in pixels.

colspan

Gives the number of columns over which the cells extend.

height

Gives the height of the cells in pixels or as a percentile of the height of the browser window.

no wrap

Gives information as to whether the normal HTML word wrap rules are valid or should be ignored.

Value	Meaning
false	The normal rules apply: text, which has come to the end of the row, will be automatically wrapped.
true	Text, which has come to the end of the row, will not be wrapped. Exceptions will only be made in the case of specified formatting (` `, `<p>`, etc).

Table 2.75 *The values for no wrap in <th>*

rowspan

Gives the number of rows over which the cells extend.

scope

States for which data cells these heading cells provide a heading.

Value	Meaning
col	This cell is the heading for all other cells in this row.
colgroup	This cell is the heading for all other cells in this row group.
row	This cell is the heading for all other cells in this row.
rowgroup	This cell is the heading for all other cells in this row group.

Table 2.76 *The values for scope in <th>*

valign

Gives the vertical alignment within the cells.

Value	Meaning
bottom	The content is aligned to the bottom.
top	The content is aligned to the top.

Table 2.77 *The values for valign in <th>*

width

Gives the width of the cells in pixels or as a percentile of the width of the browser window.

Example:

```
<table border=1>
  <caption>Browser statistic</caption>
  <tr><th>Browser</th><th>Market share</th></tr>
  <tr><td>Microsoft Internet Explorer</td><td>60.4 %</td>
  </tr>
  <tr><td>Netscape Communicator</td><td>38.5 %</td></tr>
```

```
<tr><td>Others</td><td>1.1 %</td></tr>
</table>
```

See:

```
<caption>, <col>, <colgroup>, <thead>, <tbody>, <tfoot>,
<table>, <tr>
```

2.19.7   <thead>

Tag/Attribute	2.0	3.0	3.2	4.0	Internet Explorer	Netscape
`<thead>`				X	3.0AI	
`align`				X	4.0BI	
`bgcolor`					4.0BI	
`char`				X		
`charoff`				X		
`valign`				X	4.0BI	

Defines the table head of a table.

align

Gives the horizontal alignment within the cells.

Value	Meaning
`center`	The content is centered.
`left`	The content is aligned to the left.
`right`	The content is aligned to the right.

Table 2.78   *The values for align in <thead>*

bgcolor

The background color of the cells is set here. RGB values and, for many browsers, predefined color values (see Appendix B) are the standard.

char

The code for aligning the cell content can be given here. The first appearance of this code is relevant.

charoff

Gives the gap to the defined alignment code, which has appeared for the first time in `char` in pixels.

valign

Gives the vertical alignment within the cells.

Value	Meaning
bottom	The content is aligned to the bottom.
top	The content is aligned to the top.

Table 2.79 *The values for valign in <thead>*

Example:

```
<table border=1>
  <thead>
    <tr><th colspan=2>Browser statistic</th></td>
  </thead>
  <tbody>
    <tr><th>Browser</th><th>Market share</th></tr>
    <tr><td>Microsoft Internet Explorer</td>
        <td>60.4 %</td>
    </tr>
    <tr><td>Netscape Communicator</td><td>38.5 %</td></tr>
    <tr><td>Others</td><td>1.1 %</td></tr>
  </tbody>
  <tfoot>
    <tr><td colspan=2>Status: Middle 2000</td></td>
  </tfoot>
</table>
```

See:

<caption>, <col>, <colgroup>, <table>, <tbody>, <tfoot>, <th>, <td>, <tr>

2.19.8 <title>

Tag/Attribute	2.0	3.0	3.2	4.0	Internet Explorer	Netscape
<title>	X	X	X	X	1.0	1.0

Gives the title of the HTML page in the HTML head.

See:

<base>, <isindex>, <link>, <meta>, <nextid>, <scripts>, <style>

2.19.9 <tr>

Tag/Attribute	2.0	3.0	3.2	4.0	Internet Explorer	Netscape
<tr>		X	X	X	2.0	1.1
align		X	X	X	2.0	1.1
bgcolor				X	2.0	3.0B1
bordercolor					2.0	
bordercolor-dark					2.0	
bordercolor-light					2.0	
char				X		
charoff				X		
valign		X	X	X	2.0	1.1

Defines a table row.

align

Gives the horizontal alignment within the rows.

Value	Meaning
center	The content is centered.
left	The content is aligned to the left.
right	The content is aligned to the right.

Table 2.80 *The values for align in <tr>*

bgcolor

The background color of the row is set here. RGB values and, for many browsers, predefined color values (see Appendix B) are the standard.

bordercolor

The main color for the row frame is set here. RGB values and, for many browsers, predefined color values apply (see Appendix B).

bordercolordark

The dark color for the row frame is set here in 3D. RGB values and, for many browsers, predefined color values apply (see Appendix B).

border color light

The light color for the row frame is set here in 3D. RGB values and, for many browsers, predefined color values apply (see Appendix B).

char

The code for aligning the row content can be given here. The first appearance of this code is relevant.

charoff

Gives the gap to the defined alignment code, which has appeared for the first time in char in pixels.

valign

Gives the vertical alignment within the rows.

Value	Meaning
bottom	The content is aligned to the bottom.
top	The content is aligned to the top.

Table 2.81   *The values for valign in <tr>*

Example:

```
<table border=1>
  <caption>Browser statistic</caption>
  <tr><th>Browser</th><th>Market share</th></tr>
  <tr><td>Microsoft Internet Explorer</td><td>60.4 %</td>
  </tr>
  <tr><td>Netscape Communicator</td><td>38.5 %</td></tr>
  <tr><td>Others</td><td>1.1 %</td></tr>
</table>
```

See:

<caption>, <col>, <colgroup>, <thead>, <tbody>, <tfoot>, <table>, <th>, <td>

2.19.10   <tt>

Tag/Attribute	2.0	3.0	3.2	4.0	Internet Explorer	Netscape
<tt>	X	X	X	X	1.0	1.0

The enclosed text appears in the typeface "courier".

See:

<abbr>, <b>, <big>, <blink>, <em>, <font>, <i>, <kbd>, <q>, <s>, <samp>, <small>, <strike>, <strong>, <sub>, <sup>, <u>, <var>

2.20.1 <u>

Tag/Attribute	2.0	3.0	3.2	4.0	Internet Explorer	Netscape
<u>	X	X	X	X	1.0	3.0B5

Underlines the enclosed text.

Example:

`<u>This text is underlined,</u> but this is not.`

See:

`<abbr>`, `<b>`, `<big>`, `<blink>`, `<em>`, `<font>`, `<i>`, `<kbd>`, `<q>`, `<s>`, `<samp>`, `<small>`, `<strike>`, `<strong>`, `<sub>`, `<sup>`, `<tt>`, `<var>`

2.20.2 <ul>

Tag/Attribute	2.0	3.0	3.2	4.0	Internet Explorer	Netscape
<ul>	X	X	X	X	1.0	1.0
clear		X				
compact	X	X	X	X		
type			X	X	4.0	1.0

Defines an ordered list (enumeration list).

clear

This attribute was supplemented to ensure that the user can work with images, which are moved to the left or right by the attribute `align` in `<img>`. It can be used when working with all objects, which are moved by `align`.

Value	Meaning
none	A normal word wrap is produced.
left	The line is wrapped and the next line should be inserted in such a way that the left border is free of images (or other objects).
right	The line is wrapped and the next line should be inserted in such a way that the right border is free of images (or other objects).
all	The line is wrapped and the next line should be inserted in such a way that all borders are free of images (or other objects).

Table 2.82 *The values for clear in <ul>*

compact

This sole attribute states that at least one presentation should be selected which saves space.

type

States which list points should be used.

Value	Meaning
A	A, B, C, D, ...
a	a, b, c, d, ...
I	I, II, III, IV, ...
i	i, ii, iii, iv, ...
1	1, 2, 3, 4, ...
disc	disc
square	square
circle	circle

Table 2.83 *The values for type in <ul>*

Example:

```
<ul>
  <li type="disc"> disc
  <li type="circle">circle
  <li type="square">square
</ul>
```

See:

<dd>, <dir>, <dl>, <dt>, <li>, <menu>, <ol>

2.21 V

2.21.1   <var>

Tag/Attribute	2.0	3.0	3.2	4.0	Internet Explorer	Netscape
<var>	X	X	X	X	1.0	1.0

Forms text in such a way that it can be recognized as a variable name (usually in italics).

Example:

```
Then the value of <var>x</var> is increased by one.
```

See:

```
<abbr>, <b>, <big>, <blink>, <em>, <font>, <i>, <kbd>, <q>,
<s>, <samp>, <small>, <strike>, <strong>, <sub>, <sup>,
<tt>, <u>
```

2.22 W

2.22.1 <wbr>

Tag/Attribute	2.0	3.0	3.2	4.0	Internet Explorer	Netscape
`<wbr>`					1.0	1.0

Tells the browser where a word can be wrapped, but this does not mean that it will automatically be wrapped there.

Example:

```
A ware<wbr>house has burnt down.
```

See:

```
<br>, <nobr>
```

2.23 X

2.23.1 <xml>

Tag/Attribute	2.0	3.0	3.2	4.0	Internet Explorer	Netscape
`<xml>`					5.0	
`src`					5.0	

This tag is used to insert XML text in a HTML document.

src

This attribute gives the address of the XML document.

2.23.2 <xmp>

Tag/Attribute	2.0	3.0	3.2	4.0	Internet Explorer	Netscape
`<xmp>`	X	X	X	X	1.0	1.0

The following text is reproduced word for word on the screen. The closing </xmp> tag releases this function.

2.24 !

2.24.1   <!– … –>

Tag/Attribute	2.0	3.0	3.2	4.0	Internet Explorer	Netscape
<!-- ... -->	X	X	X	X	1.0	1.0

Passages, which are framed by <!-- … -->, are ignored by the browser.

Example:

This text does not <!-- appear --> on the screen.

See:

Part III

Go Ahead!

Tips and tricks

In this section I want to introduce you to one or two topics that will be of interest.

3.1 Style sheets

You have surely realized that it can take quite a lot of effort if you want to give your homepage a unique character and maintain a certain style on every single page. For one thing you've got to write all the details several times over though they're always the same. And it's also very difficult for you when you want to change the appearance of all the pages in the same way. Just imagine you had 100 separate HTML files with a yellow background and black type. These colors suddenly no longer fit into the concept and you'd like to change them. Then you've got to modify the color definition in all 100 files. This can be quite time-consuming and is really wearing on the nerves. However there is a solution: style sheets.

A style sheet is an HTML file that defines how certain HTML elements will be displayed. Each page based on the same style file has the same visual appearance. This way we can make a small change in just one file to modify all 100 pages to the new settings.

3.1.1 Creating a style file

Before you can assign a style to Internet pages you first have to define the properties. Proceed by opening your text editor in the usual way and define the file as a style sheet. Unlike HTML files only one feature is required to turn a normal text file into a style sheet. Simply save the file as `mystyle.css` in `C:\HTML4`. So now you've created your first very own homepage style.

3.1.2 Linking in a style sheet

Let's assume you've written the following HTML file:

```
<html>
  <head>
    <title>This page uses style sheets</title>
  </head>
  <body>
    <h1>Heading 1</h1>
    <h2>Heading 2</h2>
    <h3>Heading 3</h3>
    <h4>Heading 4</h4>
    <h5>Heading 5</h5>
    Normal Text<br/>
    <a href="a.htm">A link/</a>
  </body>
</html>
```

This then looks something like:

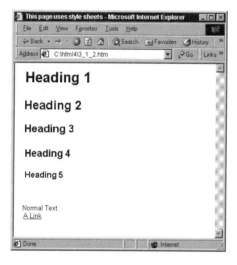

Figure 3.1 *This page is still using the default settings for Internet Explorer*

Here then we're using the fairly normal default settings. Now add the following lines in the head of your HTML file:

```
<link rel=stylesheet href="mystyle.css" type="text/css"/>
```

Now you've assigned the style sheet file `mystyle.css` to your homepage. The attributes `rel` and `type` along with the values `stylesheet` and `"text/css"` specify that you want to link in a style sheet. Specify the precise style file you want in the usual way with the `href` attribute. That's actually all there really is to say about the `<link>` tag.

Of course your homepage still won't look very different since your style file is still empty. But that's all about to change...

3.1.3   Defining your own style

In a style file we can set a very large number of homepage elements. I'll tell you a bit more about some of the elements I've picked out in the following passages:

Colors

Enter the following text in your style file:

```
h1
{
color: #800000;
}
h2
{
color: #c00000;
}
h3
{
color: #ff0000;
}
h4
{
color: #ff8080;
}
h5
{
color: #ffc0c0;
}
h6
{
color: #ffffff;
}
```

Here you've defined the appearance of the headings at levels one to six. Wherever the opening tag `<h1>` appears in your source code the color is set to dark red. Every other heading gets a lighter shade of red.

The notation is certainly a bit unusual at first. The main differences from HTML to remember are:

→ Write the tags whose appearance you want to change without brackets (`<>`).

→ Enclose changes to a tag in curly brackets ({ }).

→ In most cases the names you reference the changed attributes with will differ from those in HTML. Values follow the colon. Don't forget the semicolon after each assignment!

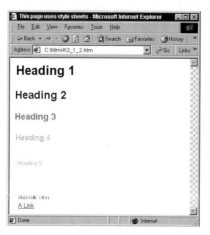

Figure 3.2 *Headings now appear in different colors*

Fonts

Changing colors is all very nice. But a variety of fonts would also be very interesting:

```
h1
{
color: #800000;
font-family: "Arial";
font-size: 25pt;
}
h2
{
color: #c00000;
font-family: "Arial";
font-size: 22pt;
}
h3
{
color: #ff0000;
font-family: "Arial";
font-size: 20pt;
}
```

```
h4
{
color: #ff8080;
font-family: "Times New Roman";
font-size: 18pt;
}
h5
{
color: #ffc0c0;
font-family: "Times New Roman";
font-size: 14pt;
}
h6
{
color: #ffffff;
font-family: "Times New Roman";
font-size: 12pt;
}
```

Here then we've given the first three headings the font (attribute: `font-fa-mily`) Arial and the last three the font `Times New Roman`. Furthermore the font size (attribute: `font-size`) gets ever smaller. The unit "pt" stands for points. But you can also type in "cm" for centimeters.

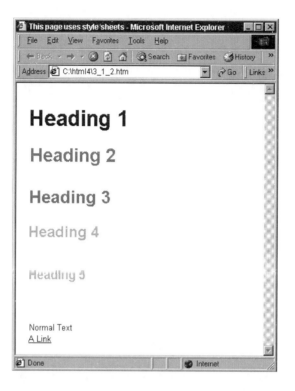

Figure 3.3 *Using predefined fonts and font sizes*

Text alignment

By means of a special text alignment feature you can add even more structure to your homepage. This way you can use `margin-left`, `margin-right` and `margin-top` to set the distance from the border. Give values in "pt" or "cm". The attribute `text-align` may take the following values:

Value	Effect
left	The text is aligned to the left edge.
center	The text is centered.
right	The text is aligned to the right edge.

Table 3.1 *Values of the text-align attribute in style files*

In addition we have the option of specifying the indent from the left edge. Do this with the attribute `text-indent`.

```
body
{
margin-left: 1cm;
```

```
margin-right: 1cm;
margin-top: 2cm;
}
h1
{
color: #800000;
font-family: "Arial";
font-size: 25pt;
}
h2
{
color: #c00000;
font-family: "Arial";
font-size: 22pt;
text-indent: 1cm;
}
h3
{
color: #ff0000;
font-family: "Arial";
font-size: 20pt;
text-indent: 2cm;
}
h4
{
color: #ff8080;
font-family: "Times New Roman";
font-size: 18pt;
text-align: center;
}
h5
{
color: #ffc0c0;
font-family: "Times New Roman";
font-size: 14pt;
text-align: center;
}
h6
{
color: #ffffff;
font-family: "Times New Roman";
font-size: 12pt;
```

```
text-align: center;
}
```

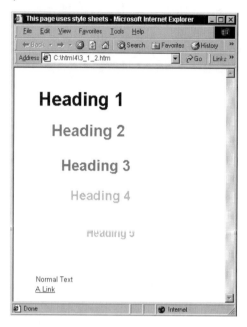

Figure 3.4 *Text alignment can also be defined in a style file*

Font style

Style files also give the option to display text in italic, bold and even with under-line or strikethrough effects. For these use `font-weight` and `text-decoration`.

Value	Effect
extra-light	The text shown is very light.
light	The text shown is light.
medium	The text shown is normal.
bold	The text shown is bold.
extra-bold	The text shown is very bold.

Table 3.2 *Values of the font-weight attribute in style files*

Value	Effect
none	Normal text.
underline	The text is underlined.
line-through	The text is struck through.

Table 3.3   *Values of the text-decoration attribute in style files*

We might include these in our example like so:

```
body
{
margin-left: 1cm;
margin-right: 1cm;
margin-top: 2cm;
}
h1
{
color: #800000;
font-family: "Arial";
font-size: 25pt;
font-weight: extra-bold;
}
h2
{
color: #c00000;
font-family: "Arial";
font-size: 22pt;
text-indent: 1cm;
font-weight: bold;
}
h3
{
color: #ff0000;
font-family: "Arial";
font-size: 20pt;
text-indent: 2cm;
font-weight: medium;
text-decoration: line-through;
}
h4
{
color: #ff8080;
font-family: "Times New Roman";
```

```
font-size: 18pt;
text-align: center;
font-style: italic;
font-weight: medium;
}
h5
{
color: #ffc0c0;
font-family: "Times New Roman";
font-size: 14pt;
text-align: center;
text-decoration: underline;
font-weight: light;
}
h6
{
color: #ffffff;
font-family: "Times New Roman";
font-size: 12pt;
text-align: center;
font-weight: extra-light;
}
```

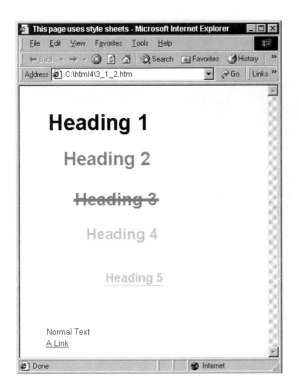

Figure 3.5 *Headings now have different set widths and some have separate font effects*

Background

To round off the functionality of style sheets I'd like to talk about adding a background. For this we only need the `background` attribute to which we can assign both a color as an RGB coding and the address of a background image. Now amend the definition of the `<body>` tag like so:

```
BODY
{
margin-left: 1cm;
margin-right: 1cm;
margin-top: 2cm;
background: url("a_bg.jpg");
}
```

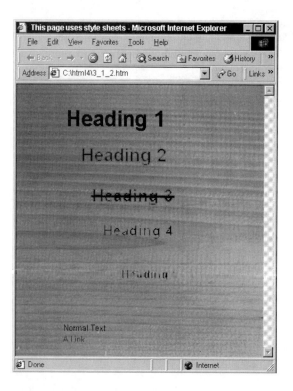

Figure 3.6 *Even the background can be defined in a style sheet*

3.1.4   Summary

Here is a summary of all the attributes once again:

Attribute	Description	Value
font-size	Defines the size of the text.	pt (points), cm (centimeters)
font-family	Defines the font.	name of the font
font-weight	Specifies the darkness or lightness of the font.	extra-light, light, medium, bold, extra-bold
font-style	Specifies the font style.	normal italic
line-height	Defines the distance between the text baselines.	pt (points), cm (centimeters), % (per cent)
color	Defines the text color.	RGB coding
text-decora-tion	Defines whether the text is underlined.	none, underline, line-through
margin-left	Specifes the distance from the left edge.	pt (points), cm (centimeters)
margin-right	Specifies the distance from the right edge.	pt (points), cm (centimeters)
margin-top	Specifies the distance from the top edge.	pt (points), cm (centimeters)
text-align	Defines the text alignment.	left, center, right
text-indent	Defines how far the text is indented from the left edge.	pt (points), cm (centimeters)
background	Specifies the background image or color.	address, RGB coding

Table 3.4   *The various attributes in style programming*

3.2   Dynamic HTML

Dynamic HTML was developed by Microsoft and appeared for the first time in Microsoft Internet Explorer 4.0. It makes your work easier if you don't have static Internet pages but want a bit more animation and interaction on your homepage.

3.2.1   What's Dynamic HTML got to offer?

Basically Dynamic HTML is a collection of JavaScripts. It offers a multitude of new possibilities for us to exploit but these would certainly go beyond the scope of this book. Here I just want to deal with one or two very interesting little features of Dynamic HTML.

3.2.2   Page transitions

When you select a link you go directly to the next page after the short time it takes for the various files to download. I'd now like to show you another way:

> **Tip** Page transitions work only with Internet Explorer 4.0 or more recent versions.

```
<html>
  <head>
    <title>Page transitions</title>
  </head>
  <body bgcolor="#000000" text="#FFFFFF">
    <h1 align="center">This is the
    start page.</h1>
    <h2 align="center">From here you go to the next
    <a href="page2.htm">page</a>.</h2>
  </body>
</html>
```

You can save this HTML file under the name `page1.htm`. It produces the follo-wing image:

Figure 3.7 *This page is the starting point for the next "experiment"*

The file page2.htm which the link refers to does not yet exist. I emphasize "not yet" because it is set out below:

```
<html>
  <head>
    <title>Page 2</title>
    <meta http-equiv="Page-Enter"
    content="revealTrans(Duration=1.0,Transition=0)">
  </head>
  <body>
    <br/>
    <br/>
    <br/>
    <br/>
    <br/>
    <br/>
    <h1 align="center">This is the second page.</h1>
    <h2 align="center">It defines the next page.</h2>
  </body>
</html>
```

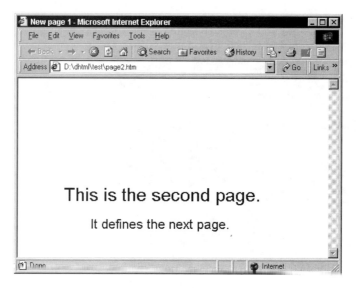

Figure 3.8 *This page defines the type of transition*

Now open the file page1.htm and click on the link to page 2.

Tip Since the illustrations take up a lot of space I've reduced them and put them side by side. Each figure has a caption saying which of the illustrations embodies which Transition. The descriptions for each then follow in turn.

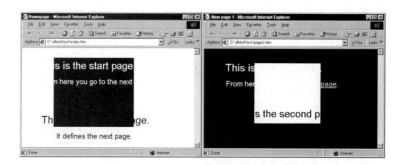

Figure 3.9 *left: 0, right: 1*

From the outside inwards (left)

```
<META http-equiv="Page-Enter" content="revealTrans(Dura-
tion=1.0,Transition=0)">
```

Using this line with the value 0 for Transition in the page head builds the page from the outside inwards.

From the inside outwards (right)

```
<META http-equiv="Page-Enter" content="revealTrans(Dura-
tion=1.0,Transition=1)">
```

Using this line with the value 1 for Transition in the page head builds the page in precisely the opposite direction, i.e. from the inside outwards.

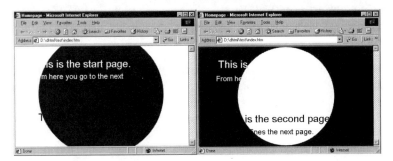

Figure 3.10 *left: 2, right: 3*

Round from the outside inwards (left)

```
<META http-equiv="Page-Enter" content="revealTrans(Dura-
tion=1.0,Transition=2)">
```

Use this line to force a transition from the outside towards the center of the screen. This page change is circular. The old page disappears to a dot at the center.

Round from the inside outwards (right)

```
<META http-equiv="Page-Enter" content="revealTrans(Dura-
tion=1.0,Transition=3)">
```

Here the new page appears first as a small dot in the center of the screen. It then keeps on expanding towards the edge of the screen until it covers the entire browser window.

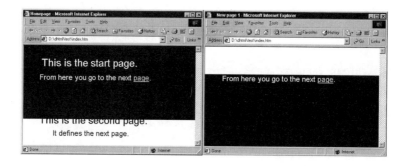

Figure 3.11 *left: 4, right: 5*

From the bottom upwards (left)

```
<META http-equiv="Page-Enter" content="revealTrans(Dura-
tion=1.0,Transition=4)">
```

Here the new page is revealed from the bottom edge of the screen upwards. If you're using an especially snappy heading the effect of surprise is particularly great when it's not visible till the end of the transition.

From the top downwards (right)

```
<META http-equiv="Page-Enter" content="revealTrans(Dura-
tion=1.0,Transition=5)">
```

This is exactly the opposite with a wipe from top to bottom. For the visitor the effect of a lively heading is one of gradually ebbing excitement.

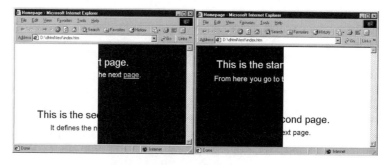

Figure 3.12 *left: 6, right: 7*

From left to right (left)

```
<META http-equiv="Page-Enter" content="revealTrans(Dura-
tion=1.0,Transition=6)">
```

Using this line with the value 6 for `Transition` in the page head builds the page from left to right.

From right to left (right)

```
<META http-equiv="Page-Enter" content="revealTrans(Dura-
tion=1.0,Transition=7)">
```

Here the new page is built from right to left. Excitement again builds up because you can't start reading straightaway but have to wait for the start of the line.

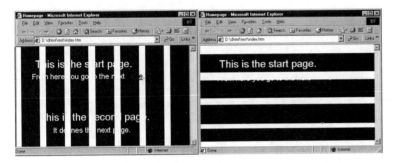

Figure 3.13 *left: 8, right: 9*

With vertical stripes (left)

```
<META http-equiv="Page-Enter" content="revealTrans(Dura-
tion=1.0,Transition=8)">
```

This creates a number of ever expanding vertical stripes. The new page only becomes readable very late on.

With horizontal stripes (right)

```
<META http-equiv="Page-Enter" content="revealTrans(Dura-
tion=1.0,Transition=9)">
```

Stripes are also used here but they run horizontally. Again they expand simultaneously. Individual lines become readable fairly quickly.

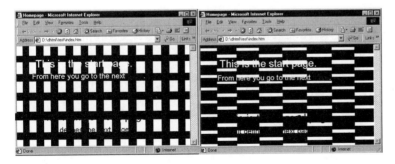

Figure 3.14 *left: 10, right: 11*

Horizontal bars (left)

```
<META http-equiv="Page-Enter" content="revealTrans(Dura-
tion=1.0,Transition=10)">
```

This creates staggered bars expanding in a horizontal direction. With this transition the new page only becomes readable fairly late on.

Vertical bars (right)

```
<META http-equiv="Page-Enter" content="revealTrans(Dura-
tion=1.0,Transition=11)">
```

This transition produces staggered bars expanding vertically.

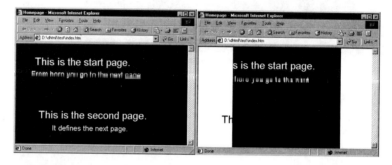

Figure 3.15 *left:12, right: 13*

Snow flurry (left)

```
<META http-equiv="Page-Enter" content="revealTrans(Dura-
tion=1.0,Transition=12)">
```

This transition is especially attractive because it resembles a snow flurry. It randomly replaces the pixels of the old page with the corresponding pixels of the new page.

From the sides inwards (right)

```
<META http-equiv="Page-Enter" content="revealTrans(Dura-
tion=1.0,Transition=13)">
```

The new page displaces the old from the sides. The old page disappears as a line in the middle of the screen.

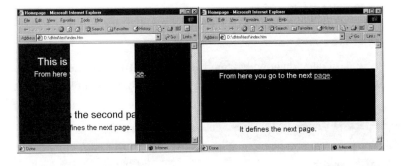

Figure 3.16 *left: 14, right: 15*

To the sides outwards (left)

```
<META http-equiv="Page-Enter" content="revealTrans(Dura-
tion=1.0,Transition=14)">
```

The reverse case lets the new page appear in the middle of the screen and expand outwards to the sides.

From top and bottom inwards (right)

```
<META http-equiv="Page-Enter" content="revealTrans(Dura-
tion=1.0,Transition=15)">
```

Using this line causes the new page to displace the old as it moves simultaneously from the top and bottom towards the middle of the screen.

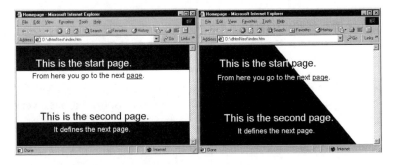

Figure 3.17 *left: 16, right: 17*

To top and bottom outwards (left)

```
<META http-equiv="Page-Enter" content="revealTrans(Dura-
tion=1.0,Transition=16)">
```

The reverse case lets the new page appear first in the middle of the screen and then run to the top and bottom edges.

From top right to bottom left (right)

```
<META http-equiv="Page-Enter" content="revealTrans(Dura-
tion=1.0,Transition=17)">
```

This displays the new page diagonally from the top right through the center to the bottom left of the screen. The effect produced broadly resembles turning over pages.

GO AHEAD!
3

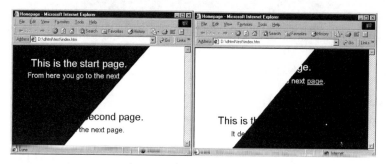

Figure 3.18 *left: 18, right: 19*

From bottom right to top left (left)

```
<META http-equiv="Page-Enter" content="revealTrans(Dura-
tion=1.0,Transition=18)">
```

This builds the new page from the bottom right to the top left. A heading only becomes visible relatively late on.

From top left to bottom right (right)

```
<META http-equiv="Page-Enter" content="revealTrans(Dura-
tion=1.0,Transition=19)">
```

Here the old page gives way to the new from top left to bottom right. Because this transition takes place from left to right and from top to bottom it has a very pleasant effect.

Figure 3.19 *left: 20, right: 21*

From bottom left to top right (left)

```
<META http-equiv="Page-Enter" content="revealTrans(Dura-
tion=1.0,Transition=20)">
```

This line accomplishes the last diagonal transition from bottom left to top right.

In horizontal layers (right)

```
<META http-equiv="Page-Enter" content="revealTrans(Dura-
tion=1.0,Transition=21)">
```

Here the new page appears line by line in random positions. The lines run horizontally.

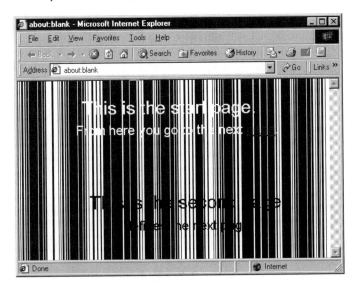

Figure 3.20 *Transition 22*

In vertical layers (above)

```
<META http-equiv="Page-Enter" content="revealTrans(Dura-
tion=1.0,Transition=22)">
```

With vertical random lines this variant suggests barcodes reminiscent of the supermarket.

At random (no illustration)

```
<META http-equiv="Page-Enter" content="revealTrans(Dura-
tion=1.0,Transition=23)">
```

Try this variant out. `Transition=23` selects one of the above transitions at random.

3.2.3   Special heading

Sometimes a small effect is enough to make a homepage especially eye-catching. As an example this small amount of JavaScript would seem to fit the bill:

```html
<html>
  <head>
    <title>Dynamic HTML</title>
    <script language="JavaScript">
    <!--
      function title_onmouseover()
      {
        pgtitle.style.color = "yellow"
      }
      function title_onmouseout()
      {
        pgtitle.style.color = "black"
      }
    //-->
    </script>
  </head>
  <body>
    <h1><a id=pgtitle onmouseover="title_onmouseover();"
    onmouseout="title_onmouseout();" >
    Please move the mouse over this
    heading.</a></h1>
  </body>
</html>
```

If we take a look at the page the following image appears:

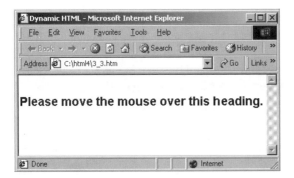

Figure 3.21   *The heading still looks quite normal ...*

Now move the mouse over the heading.

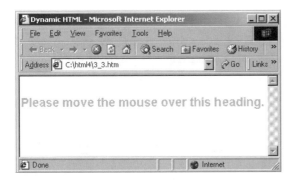

Figure 3.22   *... but with Dynamic HTML the color changes when the mouse moves over the heading*

Tip Dynamic HTML is very versatile. You can for instance design very interesting page transitions. There are a variety of other things it can do, though these go beyond the scope of this book.

3.3 Useful JavaScripts

Here I've listed a few JavaScripts for you that'll turn out very useful for your Internet pages:

3.3.1 Date of last update

If we want to tell the visitor at a glance whether something has changed on the page since the last visit, we can display the date that the site was last updated. If you'd like to save yourself the trouble of logging every change you can use the following simple script at the appropriate place in your HTML text:

```
<script language="JavaScript">
  <!--
    document.write("This page was last updated on: " + doc-
ument.lastModified);
  //-->
</script>
```

If you look at the result with a browser the following image appears:

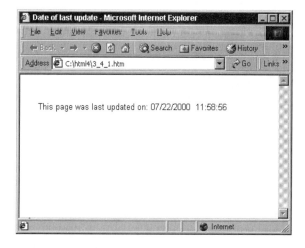

Figure 3.23 *A JavaScript calculates the date of last update*

How does the browser suddenly know when the page has been changed? You know of course that every file saves the date created and the date modified. The source code shown above retrieves precisely this information from the current HTML file and writes it automatically onto the screen.

3.3.2 Compatibility script

In the section on music we've already seen the problem of different browsers. Some use different tags to express the same thing. If you want Netscape to play music in the background <embed> is necessary. Internet Explorer also has the side effect when using hidden=true of leaving the screen blank at the place where the application would appear. Instead it would therefore be better to use

`<bgsound>` but Netscape doesn't understand this. If you want to resolve this conflict then once again add a JavaScript:

```
<script language="JavaScript">
  <!--
    if(navigator.userAgent.indexOf("Macintosh") == -1)
    {
      if(navigator.appName == "Netscape")
      document.writeln("<embed src=a_song.mid
autostart=true hidden=true>");
      else document.writeln("<bgsound src=a_song.mid>");
    }
  //-->
</script>
```

This script first checks if the visitor is using a Macintosh. If this is the case then no music will play at all. Otherwise it tests whether it's dealing with Netscape or Internet Explorer. Depending on the result it then includes in the HTML text either the line

```
<embed src=a_song.mid autostart=true hidden=true>
```

in the case of Netscape or

```
<bgsound src=a_song.mid>
```

in the case of Internet Explorer. Note that you mustn't use quotation marks as these have already been opened for the script.

You can modify this script at any time to suit your purposes if you have to create different command lines for various browsers.

3.3.3   Status line marquee

If you want to make a good impression add the following script to your page:

```
<html>
  <head>
    <script language="JavaScript">
      <!--
        function status_line(x)
        {
          var msg  = "This book is published in the
Nitty-Gritty series of the Addison Wesley Publishing Com-
pany.";
var out = " ";
          var c    = 1;
          var e    = 120;
```

```
          if (x > e)
          {
            x--;
            var cmd="status_line(" + x + ")";
            timerTwo=window.setTimeout(cmd,100);
          }
          else if (x <= e && x > 0)
          {
            for (c=0 ; c < x ; c++)
            {
              out+=" ";
            }
            out+=msg;
            x--;
            var cmd="status_line(" + x + ")";
            window.status=out;
            timerTwo=window.setTimeout(cmd,100);
          }
          else if (x <= 0)
          {
            if (-x < msg.length)
            {
              out+=msg.substring(-x,msg.length);
              x--;
              var cmd="status_line(" + x + ")";
              window.status=out;
              timerTwo=window.setTimeout(cmd,100);
            }
            else
            {
              window.status=" ";
              timerTwo=
              window.setTimeout("status_line("+e+")",100);
            }
          }
        }
      }
      // -->
    </script>
    <title>A marquee</title>
  </head>
  <body onload=
  "timerONE=window.setTimeout('status_line(120)',100);">
```

```
    <h1>Please watch the status bar!</h1>
  </body>
</html>
```

This program causes the text assigned to the variable `msg` to appear in the status bar of the browser as a marquee.

| A marquee - Microsoft Internet Explorer | _ □ × |

File   Edit   View   Favorites   Tools   Help

← Back · → · ⊗ ⓘ ⌂ | ⊕ Search ▣ Favorites ⊛ History | ▣ · ⊜ ▤ ▤

Address ⦿ C:\html4\3_4_2.htm ▼ ∂ Go ‖ Links »

Please watch the status bar!

⦿ This book is published in the Nitty-Gritty series   ⊕ Internet

Figure 3.24 *With a marquee like this in the status bar you'll amaze any visitor to your homepage*

Note that you have to start this script using the call

```
onload="timerONE=window.setTime-
out('status_line(120)',100);"
in <body>.
```

At this point I'd like to draw your attention to some Internet pages which might be of interest as regards HTML 4 and this book.

3.4 Some interesting pages on the web

3.4.1 Browsers

Microsoft Internet Explorer

Microsoft Internet Explorer is without doubt the most popular browser. You can download new versions or obtain information on new plug-ins and updates here.

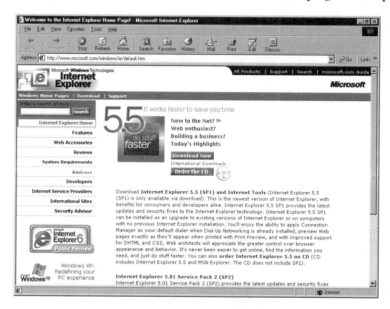

Figure 3.25 *www.microsoft.com/windows/ie/*

Netscape Navigator

The second most popular browser is Netscape Navigator. Here you can also obtain updates and further information.

Figure 3.26 *www.netscape.com/*

3.4.2   HTML

Here is a list of interesting pages on HTML.

W3C

The World Wide Web Consortium (W3C) is responsible for the further development of HTML. Here you will find new references and similar material.

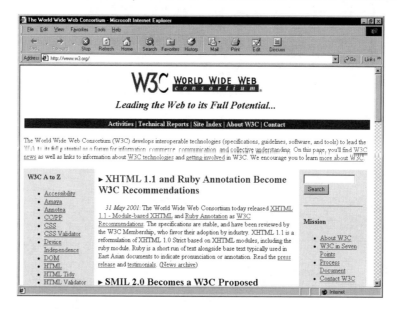

Figure 3.27   *www.w3c.org/*

Self HTML

If you can understand German then you will find a very good online introduction to HTML and other Internet languages in "Self HTML".

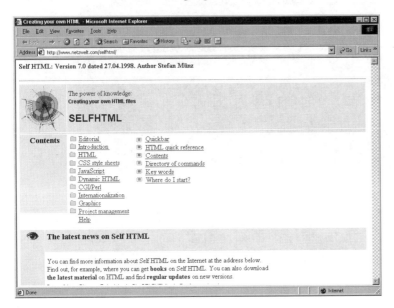

Figure 3.28 *www.netzwelt.com/selfhtml*

Developer Zone

In Developer Zone you'll find a lot of useful information on HTML, XML and CSS.

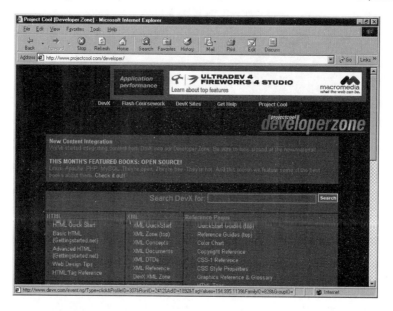

Figure 3.29   *www.projectcool.com/developer*

WebCoder

If you are looking for references or examples of Dynamic HTML or JavaScript then check out WebCoder.

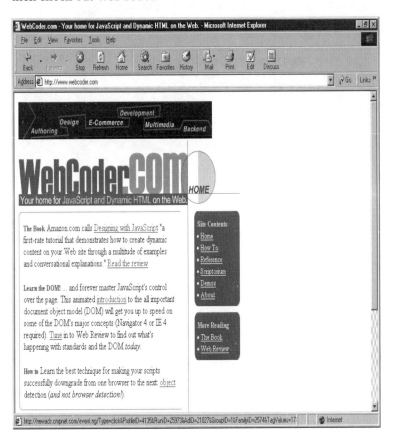

Figure 3.30 *http://webcoder.com/*

Site Experts

Site Experts deals with HTML, XML and CSS. It's well worth a visit.

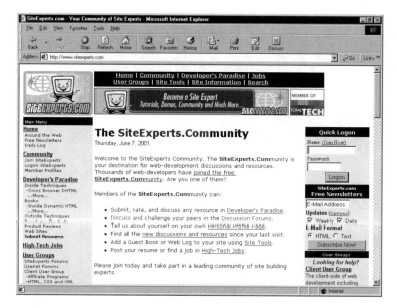

Figure 3.31   *www.siteexperts.com/*

3.4.3 About this book

Addison-Wesley

This book is published by Addison-Wesley which of course has its own website. Here you will find textbooks written by professionals for professionals.

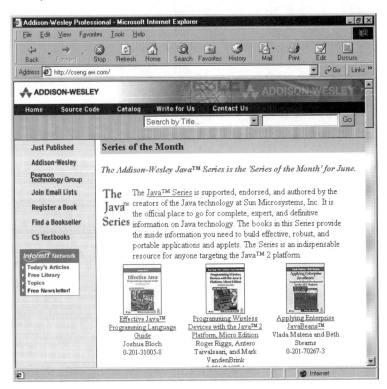

Figure 3.32 *http://cseng.aw.com/*

y final tip ... ... is the following: you never stop learning. Therefore you should always look at the source code of Internet pages that contain elements whose appearance you can't explain. This way you'll keep your knowledge of HTML up to date. With Microsoft Internet Explorer you've always got the opportunity to look at the source code by clicking the right mouse button and selecting "View Source".

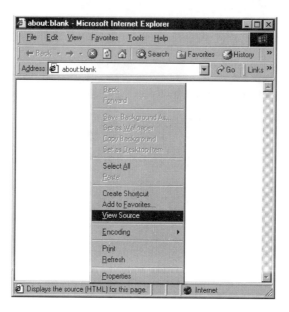

Figure 3.33 *Use this option to view the source code of a page even if it's in a frame*

If you want to look at the text of a page which creates frames simply go to the menu item View Source.

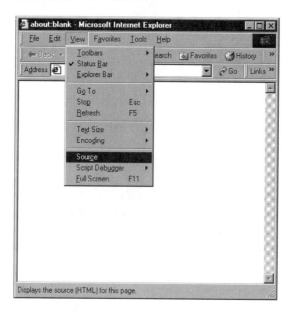

Figure 3.34 *How to access the source code of a page creating frames*

Appendix

A Character references for special characters

Character	Character reference
	&#32;
"	&quot;
&	&amp;
<	&lt;
>	&gt;
@	&#64;
{	&#123;
}	&#125;
~	&#126;
¡	&#161;
¢	&#162;
£	&#163;
¤	&#164;
¥	&#165;
©	&#169;
	&#172;
®	&#174;
°	&#176;
±	&#177;
µ	&#181;
¼	&#188;
½	&#189;
¾	&#190;
¿	&#191;
À	&Agrave;

Character	Character reference
Á	&Aacute;
Â	&Acirc;
Ã	&Atilde;
Ä	&Auml;
Å	&Aring;
Æ	&AElig;
Ç	&Ccedil;
È	&Egrave;
É	&Eacute;
Ê	&Ecirc;
Ë	&Euml;
Ì	&Igrave;
Í	&Iacute;
Î	&Icirc;
Ï	&Iuml;
Ñ	&Ntilde;
Ò	&Ograve;
Ó	&Oacute;
Ô	&Ocirc;
Õ	&Otilde;
Ö	&Ouml;
Ø	&Oslash;
Ù	&Ugrave;
Ú	&Uacute;
Û	&Ucirc;
Ü	&Uuml;
Ý	&Yacute;
Þ	&THORN;
ß	&szlig;
à	&agrave;
á	&aacute;
â	&acirc;
ã	&atilde;
ä	&auml;
å	&aring;
æ	&aelig;
ç	&ccedil;
è	&egrave;

Character	Character reference
é	é
ê	â
ë	ë
ì	ì
í	í
î	î
ï	ï
ð	ð
ñ	ñ
ò	ò
ó	ó
ô	ô
õ	õ
ö	ö
ø	ø
ù	ù
ú	ú
û	û
ü	ü
ý	ý
ÿ	ÿ

Table A.1 *Representation of special characters using character references.*

B Predefined color values

The following table gives all the predefined colors in JavaScript along with their RGB values.

Color	Red	Green	Blue
aliceblue	F0	F8	FF
antiquewhite	FA	EB	D7
aqua	00	FF	FF
aquamarine	7F	FF	D4
azure	F0	FF	FF
beige	F5	F5	DC
bisque	FF	E4	C4
black	00	00	00
blanchedalmond	FF	EB	CD

Color	Red	Green	Blue
blue	00	00	FF
blueviolet	8A	2B	E2
brown	A5	2A	2A
burlywood	DE	B8	87
cadetblue	5F	9E	A0
chartreuse	7F	FF	00
chocolate	D2	69	1E
coral	FF	7F	50
cornflowerblue	64	95	ED
cornsilk	FF	F8	DC
crimson	DC	14	3C
cyan	00	FF	FF
darkblue	00	00	8B
darkcyan	00	8B	8B
darkgoldenrod	B8	86	0B
darkgray	A9	A9	A9
darkgreen	00	64	00
darkkhaki	BD	B7	6B
darkmagenta	8B	00	8B
darkolivegreen	55	6B	2F
darkorange	FF	8C	00
darkorchid	99	32	CC
darkred	8B	00	00
darksalmon	E9	96	7A
darkseagreen	8F	BC	8F
darkslateblue	48	3D	8B
darkslategray	2F	4F	4F
darkturquoise	00	CE	D1
darkviolet	94	00	D3
deeppink	FF	14	93
deepskyblue	00	BF	FF
dimgray	69	69	69
dodgerblue	1E	90	FF
firebrick	B2	22	22
floralwhite	FF	FA	F0
forestgreen	22	8B	22
fuchsia	FF	00	FF
gainsboro	DC	DC	DC

Color	Red	Green	Blue
ghostwhite	F8	F8	FF
gold	FF	D7	00
goldenrod	DA	A5	20
gray	80	80	80
green	00	80	00
greenyellow	AD	FF	2F
honeydew	F0	FF	F0
hotpink	FF	69	B4
indianred	CD	5C	5C
indigo	4B	00	82
ivory	FF	FF	F0
khaki	F0	E6	8C
lavender	E6	E6	FA
lavenderblush	FF	F0	F5
lawngreen	7C	FC	00
lemonchiffon	FF	FA	CD
lightblue	AD	D8	E6
lightcoral	F0	80	80
lightcyan	E0	FF	FF
lightgoldenrodyellow	FA	FA	D2
lightgreen	90	EE	90
lightgrey	D3	D3	D3
lightpink	FF	B6	C1
lightsalmon	FF	A0	7A
lightseagreen	20	B2	AA
lightskyblue	87	CE	FA
lightslategray	77	88	99
lightsteelblue	B0	C4	DE
lightyellow	FF	FF	E0
lime	00	FF	00
limegreen	32	CD	32
linen	FA	F0	E6
magenta	FF	00	FF
maroon	80	00	00
mediumaquamarine	66	CD	AA
mediumblue	00	00	CD
mediumorchid	BA	55	D3
mediumpurple	93	70	DB

B

Color	Red	Green	Blue
mediumseagreen	3C	B3	71
mediumslateblue	7B	68	EE
mediumspringgreen	00	FA	9A
mediumturquoise	48	D1	CC
mediumvioletred	C7	15	85
midnightblue	19	19	70
mintcream	F5	FF	FA
mistyrose	FF	E4	E1
moccasin	FF	E4	B5
navajowhite	FF	DE	AD
navy	00	00	80
oldlace	FD	F5	E6
olive	80	80	00
olivedrab	6B	8E	23
orange	FF	A5	00
orangered	FF	45	00
orchid	DA	70	D6
palegoldenrod	EE	E8	AA
palegreen	98	FB	98
paleturquoise	AF	EE	EE
palevioletred	DB	70	93
papayawhip	FF	EF	D5
peachpuff	FF	DA	B9
peru	CD	85	3F
pink	FF	C0	CB
plum	DD	A0	DD
powderblue	B0	E0	E6
purple	80	00	80
red	FF	00	00
rosybrown	BC	8F	8F
royalblue	41	69	E1
saddlebrown	8B	45	13
salmon	FA	80	72
sandybrown	F4	A4	60
seagreen	2E	8B	57
seashell	FF	F5	EE
sienna	A0	52	2D
silver	C0	C0	C0

Color	Red	Green	Blue
skyblue	87	CE	EB
slateblue	6A	5A	CD
slategray	70	80	90
snow	FF	FA	FA
springgreen	00	FF	7F
steelblue	46	82	B4
tan	D2	B4	8C
teal	00	80	80
thistle	D8	BF	D8
tomato	FF	63	47
turquoise	40	E0	D0
violet	EE	82	EE
wheat	F5	DE	B3
white	FF	FF	FF
whitesmoke	F5	F5	F5
yellow	FF	FF	00
yellowgreen	9A	CD	32

Table B.1 *Predefined colors in HTML 4*

C The hexadecimal numbers

D	H	D	H	D	H	D	H	D	H	D	H	D	H	D	H
0	00	16	10	32	20	48	30	64	40	80	50	96	60	112	70
1	01	17	11	33	21	49	31	65	41	81	51	97	61	113	71
2	02	18	12	34	22	50	32	66	42	82	52	98	62	114	72
3	03	19	13	35	23	51	33	67	43	83	53	99	63	115	73
4	04	20	14	36	24	52	34	68	44	84	54	100	64	116	74
5	05	21	15	37	25	53	35	69	45	85	55	101	65	117	75
6	06	22	16	38	26	54	36	70	46	86	56	102	66	118	76
7	07	23	17	39	27	55	37	71	47	87	57	103	67	119	77
8	08	24	18	40	28	56	38	72	48	88	58	104	68	120	78
9	09	25	19	41	29	57	39	73	49	89	59	105	69	121	79
10	0A	26	1A	42	2A	58	3A	74	4A	90	5A	106	6A	122	7A
11	0B	27	1B	43	2B	59	3B	75	4B	91	5B	107	6B	123	7B
12	0C	28	1C	44	2C	60	3C	76	4C	92	5C	108	6C	124	7C
13	0D	29	1D	45	2D	61	3D	77	4D	93	5D	109	6D	125	7D
14	0E	30	1E	46	2E	62	3E	78	4E	94	5E	110	6E	126	7E
15	0F	31	1F	47	2F	63	3F	79	4F	95	5F	111	6F	127	7F

D	H	D	H	D	H	D	H	D	H	D	H	D	H	D	H
128	80	144	90	160	A0	176	B0	192	C0	208	D0	224	E0	240	F0
129	81	145	91	161	A1	177	B1	193	C1	209	D1	225	E1	241	F1
130	82	146	92	162	A2	178	B2	194	C2	210	D2	226	E2	242	F2
131	83	147	93	163	A3	179	B3	195	C3	211	D3	227	E3	243	F3
132	84	148	94	164	A4	180	B4	196	C4	212	D4	228	E4	244	F4
133	85	149	95	165	A5	181	B5	197	C5	213	D5	229	E5	245	F5
134	86	150	96	166	A6	182	B6	198	C6	214	D6	230	E6	246	F6
135	87	151	97	167	A7	183	B7	199	C7	215	D7	231	E7	247	F7
136	88	152	98	168	A8	184	B8	200	C8	216	D8	232	E8	248	F8
137	89	153	99	169	A9	185	B9	201	C9	217	D9	233	E9	249	F9
138	8A	154	9A	170	AA	186	BA	202	CA	218	DA	234	EA	250	FA
139	8B	155	9B	171	AB	187	BB	203	CB	219	DB	235	EB	251	FB
140	8C	156	9C	172	AC	188	BC	204	CC	220	DC	236	EC	252	FC
141	8D	157	9D	173	AD	189	BD	205	CD	221	DD	237	ED	253	FD
142	8E	158	9E	174	AE	190	BE	206	CE	222	DE	238	EE	254	FE
143	8F	159	9F	175	AF	191	BF	207	CF	223	DF	239	EF	255	FF

D Glossary

Here I've brought together all the terms I've referred to in the book that may need further explanation.

Address

To access any service in the Internet you'll need an address. This can have many formats. An e-mail address might look like: `name@provider.com`. But to reach a homepage you'd use something like: `http://www.provider.com/`

Anchor

Anchor is the term given to the image or text you have to click to reach the page the link points to.

Attribute

An attribute is what you assign to a tag in HTML to describe more accurately the properties of the element created. For example, if you create a horizontal rule with `<hr/>` you can define its thickness using the attribute `size`.

```
<hr size="4">
```

This command produces a much stronger line than `<hr/>` alone.

Operating system

On startup every computer has to call a basic program that tells it how to respond to inputs and operate the hardware. We call this program an operating system. The most popular versions are MS-DOS, OS/2, Windows 95/98/NT/2000, MacOS, Linux and Unix.

Browser

A browser is a program that converts HTML into a graphical image and interprets the input of the user so allowing them to surf the Internet. The most popular browsers are Netscape Navigator and Microsoft Internet Explorer.

CGI

CGI (Common Gateway Interface) is a standard that defines an interface between computers. Typically it's used to define the data transfer of CGI scripts.

Service provider

A service provider makes the connection between the customer and the Internet. You dial in via a modem or ISDN to your service provider who then transmits all the data you've requested to your computer.

Download

This is the transfer of a file from another computer to your own.

Dynamic HTML

Dynamic HTML is an extension of HTML that enables you to program animations and many other elements with HTML.

Editor

See Text editor.

E-mail

In everyday life you'll certainly have written a letter. In exactly the same way you can also send mail over the Internet. You type in the address of the recipient and add your text. Within a few minutes (sometimes just seconds) the letter is with the recipient as a file. It's therefore much quicker than sending a letter and what's more there's no postage to pay. This is called an e-mail.

Hard disk

A computer stores the operating system as well as other programs on a hard disk. This hardware is comparable with a floppy disk though much faster and bigger.

FTP

When we speak of FTP in connection with the Internet we mean the "File Transfer Protocol". Computers communicate with one another in various languages (protocols). This one was developed specially for exchanging data on the Internet. Through the use of an FTP site it's no problem to access large file archives of companies, universities and other institutions.

Guest access

Many service providers make software available to their members. So that only members actually have access to it, user ID and a password are requested when establishing the connection. A lot of data however is also released to Internet users who aren't members. These visitors can then register using the name "Guest" or "Anonymous". Typing in a password is often unnecessary though. In some cases the e-mail address of the guest is designated as the password. But you'll be given plenty of warning.

Hardware

Computer hardware consists of the computer itself together with all its cards, the monitor, keyboard, mouse, printer and all the other devices connected to it.

Homepage

A homepage mainly consists of a number of files that any Internet user can look at. HTML is the language most often used to write a homepage, which is displayed using a browser program. Homepages give information about individuals, companies, universities and other institutions.

HTML

HTML (Hypertext Markup Language) was developed by Tim Berners-Lee to allow people to publish work that could be accesible to anyone else on a network, without facing compatibility problems regarding what Operating System software or format you use. It controls the programming of links and simplifies the construction of tables, forms and lists. HTML even allows the use of multimedia elements like videos and music.

HTTP

The Hypertext Transfer Protocol (HTTP) is used for the transfer of files based on HTML. Homepages are therefore mainly transferred using this protocol.

The Internet

The Internet is a worldwide network of computers. Originally it was developed by the military to maintain an operational communications network in the event of failure of some of their computers. Since then though it's also become an increasingly important medium for companies and private individuals.

ISDN

Major telecom companies now offer not only the conventional analogue telephone connections but also digital ISDN connections. This system converts voice signals first into a digital pattern and then at the other end back into audio signals. Since programs and files are stored and transferred digital ISDN is a fast way to transfer data.

Java

Programs written in Java are transferred over the Internet and then run on your computer. This programming language was developed specially for the Internet.

Body

The body of an HTML file lists all the data, images and other elements that will later appear in the browser window. Also defined here are the alignment and configuration of these elements.

Head

The head of an HTML file includes the title of the page.

Link

A link is a connection between two Internet pages. When you select a link on the current page you go the target page.

Modem

A modem is required to transmit data over a telephone line. This piece of hardware converts data into audio signals. The other end also has a modem which reverses this process. A modem therefore supports two-way conversion.

Network

A network is a group of computers exchanging data with each other. The Internet is therefore a huge network.

Pixel

A pixel is the smallest point you can display on the screen. If you're using a screen resolution of 800 x 600 pixels you can display 480 000 pixels.

Protocol

During data transfer protocols can check if all the data has arrived and whether it may have changed on the way due perhaps to some kind of fault.

Source code

Text which describes an HTML file is called source code.

Server

A computer that stores data to make it available for other computers in the network is called a server.

Software

All programs and data you can save are called software.

Special characters

All characters not belonging to the letters A to Z or the numbers 0 to 9 are called special characters.

Storage space

We require storage space for saving data. It can be main memory or hard disk capacity.

Dedicated line

We call a permanent connection between two computers a dedicated line.

Surfing

"Surfing" means going from one web page to another.

Style sheet

A style sheet is a format template that you can call on in many HTML pages. This saves a great deal of work because you only need to make changes in just one file.

Tag

An HTML file consists of normal text. To display other elements it's necessary to separate these elements from the text. We use tags enclosed in brackets to do this.

Telnet

Telnet is a protocol that enables you to execute and control programs on other computers. It's text based.

Text editor

The purpose of a text editor is to create and modify text files. The Windows program "Notepad" is a text editor.

Upload

This is the opposite of download. Here you transfer a file from your own computer to the other computer.

URL

See Address.

The World Wide Web (WWW)

The "World Wide Web" is the most prominent internet service of today. It is the 'face' of the internet that most of the public will be familiar with. It's not the most used part of the internet — that crown is worn by email — more people are sending emails than ever before. However, for most people, the internet is (erroneously) synonymous with the web. The web is the visual and audible and interactive 'front end' for a growing number of services and businesses, as well as providing a virtual space for countless individual's published home pages.

Index